Secrets
of
Effective
Leadership

Secrets
of
Effective
Leadership

Fred A. Manske, Jr.

LEADERSHIP EDUCATION AND DEVELOPMENT, INC.
COLUMBIA, TN.

Revised 1990

Published by Leadership Education and Development, Inc.
1116 West 7th Street, Suite 175, Columbia, TN. 38401.

First Edition, 1987
Second Edition, 1990

Printed in the United States of America

Library of Congress Cataloging-in-Publication Data

Manske, Fred A., 1939-
    Secrets of effective leadership / Fred A. Manske, Jr. — 2nd ed.

    Includes bibliographical references and index.
    ISBN 0-943703-03-4 : $19.95
    1. Leadership.   2. Executive ability.   I. Title.
HD57.7.M37   1990
658.4'09—dc20

Contents

Contents

Acknowledgements

People develop their leadership skills by observing and emulating competent leaders and by being coached.

Over the years I have been fortunate to work for a number of outstanding leaders. Each person in a unique way contributed to the development of my leadership style. At Sealtest Foods, Bill Wade, Martin Downs and Duane Malm coached me through my early years in management. Most of my middle management career was spent at Eastern Airlines where I developed line and staff skills under the direction of George Bowers, Rick Rivenbank, Bob Walcott and, most of all, Frank Borman.

For the past thirteen years I have been associated with the unique company Federal Express and its chief operating officers Art Bass, Pete Willmott, Jim Barksdale and its innovative leader Fred Smith.

To all these gentlemen I express my deepest gratitude for the time and interest they invested in me.

There are two other significant people in my life who have been instrumental in shaping my leadership skills. They are my father, Fred A. Manske, Sr. and my father-in-law, Donald C. Harrison. In different but important ways each of them set examples of leadership worth emulating.

Finally, numerous individuals assisted me in the project of writing *Secrets of Effective Leadership*. Dr. George Jensen, Robert McEmber, Barbara Bekis and Jeanne Thurman Cross assisted in the editing. Janice Means worked tirelessly to type and retype numerous drafts of the book. Joy Walker Rhodes was instrumental in coordinating the printing and publication activities. And most of all, I thank my family (Donna and the children Fred III, Don and Cindy) whose love and understanding have given me strength to continually focus on my career. Together, they have provided a supportive, happy home where we have shared the experiences of the corporate life. Without them, the book would never have been possible.

Preface

Secrets of Effective Leadership: A Practical Guide to Success had its inception in the early 1970's when Mr. Manske worked for Eastern Airlines as Director of Training. He noticed that the management trainees were thirsty to learn from the experiences of respected leaders who made classroom presentations. The trainees were particularly interested in the stories of the leaders' past victories and failures. This led Mr. Manske to begin recording his own leadership experiences. Over the years he collected numerous anecdotes and inspirational quotations from outstanding leaders, past and present, from all walks of life.

Secrets of Effective Leadership sets the example for the highest standards of honesty and integrity in leaders at a time when such attributes are desperately needed in organizations. People long to work for ethical, principled leaders who put the needs of the organization above their own.

The philosophy of the author is that people should be treated fairly and with dignity **not** for what it will gain the leader, but because it is the right and decent thing to do.

Secrets of Effective Leadership is written from the perspective of someone who has been there in the trenches — at the front lines of the operating functions of business. Mr. Manske knows what it is like to work under constant pressure to improve quality, sales and profits at higher and higher levels each year. He has worked with strong international unions and appreciates the difficulties of trying to lead employee groups during periods of rapid growth and severe economic downturns. This extensive hands-on experience helped the author identify and describe the secrets of leadership necessary for success in today's challenging business world.

The quick reference format is a unique aspect of the book. The chapters are designed to stand on their own. Readers can use *Secrets of Effective Leadership* as a **handbook** for guidance to solve leadership problems when they occur.

Secrets of Effective Leadership emphasizes **practical** leadership principles and strategies that can be applied daily to inspire and energize people in organizations. Valuable ideas are presented on **how** to unleash your full leadership potential by (1) building on your leadership strengths and (2) managing both stress and your personal life.

Thoughtful study and application of the philosophies, principles and ideas in *Secrets of Effective Leadership* can be your guide to success!

Introduction

There is a growing respect for leadership wisdom and experience in the corporate world. While management techniques, systems and programs were revered a few years ago, a premium is now placed on leadership — obtaining excellence from people. For years, management placed insufficient attention on developing employees and inspiring them to be fully productive.

The trend toward increased emphasis on leadership is a reaction to the massive change that is occurring in the way business is conducted world-wide. The United States was once a self-sufficient national economy. Now we are part of an interdependent global economy.[1] The only way to successfully compete in such an economic environment is to produce high quality products and services at low cost.

This goal requires both sophisticated production systems and the total dedication of employees to excellence — 100% defect-free or error-free work. Excellence in an organization does not occur spontaneously. It is inspired, nurtured and sustained by competent leaders.

Secrets of Effective Leadership was written with one purpose in mind: to contribute to the development of business leaders by providing **practical** advice on how to obtain excellence from people.

I

What is Leadership?

The art of leadership can be defined in many ways. Here are a few definitions that are as appropriate today as they were in the past.

Harry Truman: A leader is a man who has the ability to get other people to do what they don't want to do and like it!

Field Marshall Montgomery: Leadership is the capacity and the will to rally men and women to a common purpose and the character which inspires confidence.

Vince Lombardi: Coaches who can outline plays on the blackboard are a dime a dozen. The ones who succeed are those who can get inside their players and motivate them.

To me, a leader is a visionary that energizes others. This definition of leadership has two key dimensions: (a) creating a vision of the future and (b) inspiring people to make the vision reality.

Outstanding leaders are future oriented. They love to dream about what could be and to involve others in their dreams.

When a corporate leader has vision, he or she has an image or idea of what his or her organization should do in the future and how it should get there. In her classic management book, *Dynamic Administration,* Mary Parker Follett commented on this vital aspect of leadership by saying, "The most successful leader of all is the one who sees another picture not actualized."[1]

Fredrick W. Smith had such a vision in the early 1970's. In a term paper for an economics course at Yale University he explained his vision of an air express system that would provide overnight and nationwide delivery of urgent packages. At the time that vision seemed impractical and farfetched. In fact,

3

Smith's economics professor gave him a "C" on the term paper. Undaunted, Smith used the ideas formulated in that "C" paper to create an A + company — Federal Express. Today the Federal Express Corporation has the reputation of being an exceptional company. It is the world's largest air express and air freight carrier and is ranked in the top ten of the best places to work in America.[2]

Those that create, lead!

Another business leader who envisioned a product that significantly impacted America was Allen H. Neuharth, former chairman of the Gannet Corporation, a major publishing firm. His vision was that of a **national** newspaper delivered to homes and news stands early each morning. Neuharth's dream was not to produce a traditional daily paper. He believed there was a whole new generation of readers who wanted the news presented in concise format utilizing colorful charts and graphs to explain world and national news, lifestyles, sports and finance.

When the first edition of *USA Today* reached the streets on September 15, 1982, many people doubted it would succeed. As the annual losses grew, it appeared that the skeptics were right. Yet, Neuharth refused to abandon his dream of a unique newspaper. Finally, in late 1987, *USA Today* became profitable and obtained over five million readers — the largest daily readership in America.

Martin Luther King, who led the great crusade for civil rights from 1955 to 1968, epitomized a leader with great vision and the tenacity to move ahead at all costs. Despite being jailed several times, stabbed and stoned, King persisted in his efforts to fulfill his dream of a world of racial equality and improved living conditions for the poor.

Like small creeks that grow into mighty rivers, the dreams of leaders eventually shape the course of history.

No one who was at the Washington Monument the afternoon of August 28, 1963, will ever forget the conclusion of King's speech before a crowd estimated to be over 250,000. Biographer Lerone Bennett, Jr. captured the electricity and emotion of the moment:

> Digging deep within himself, picking up bits and pieces of speeches dating back to 1956, he began to improvise, rolling out long legato phrases that brought

cheers like thunderous waves . . . over and over again King repeated, ''I have a dream . . .'' and the throng, electrified, rose en masse, screaming, cheering and crying, pushing him to ascending heights of revelations and discovery.[3]

Vision is therefore the first critical dimension of effective leadership. Without vision there is little or no sense of purpose in an organization. Efforts drift aimlessly. The loss of purpose leads to a lack of coordination between work units and divisive infighting among executives.

Visions and intellectual strategies alone are insufficient to motivate and energize people at work. Sustained results come only if employees buy into a vision; they must believe that the leader's vision is **their** vision. Only then will they accept responsibility for achieving it. Herein lies the second key dimension of leadership: inspiring or energizing employees to perform at their best individually and collectively.

It is not an easy task to get people to perform beyond what they think possible, to routinely give an extra ten to twenty percent. Nor is it a simple procedure to mold a group of diverse individuals into a tight-knit team dedicated to excellence. Accomplishing both of these missions is the ultimate challenge of leadership and the primary focus of this book.

John Naisbitt terms the energization of people to strive for a single vision ''alignment.''[4] In its highest form alignment exists when groups or teams of employees are totally dedicated to accomplishing the mission at hand and collaborate together unselfishly toward that end. At this point the goals of the organization and the individual are meshed or congruent.

The many ways that leaders energize others will be discussed in the following chapters. In general, however, leaders create a positive attitude or force in their organizations. They do this through the strength of their commitment and vision, by their personal vigor and by the creation of the feeling that good things are happening. Once this positive force begins, others in the group are stirred to action; soon an avalanche of enthusiasm is underway. Leadership in this sense provides hope and meaning for employees; the employees begin to believe that their

Outstanding leaders appeal to the hearts of their followers — not their minds.

One of the greatest gifts we can give others is hope.

own future goals can be realized through the organization's goals.

So far leadership has been defined in terms of its two key dimensions: a vision of the company's purpose and the energization of people to achieve that purpose. Further understanding is available by comparing the information on leadership and management in the following table.

COMPARISON OF LEADERS AND MANAGERS

Leaders Tend to	Managers Tend to . . . .
Stress relationships with others, values and commitment — the emotional and spiritual aspects of the organization.	Stress organization, coordination and control of resources (e.g., plant, equipment and people).
Create and articulate a vision of what the organization could achieve in the long run.	Focus on the achievement of short-term objectives and goals.
Move the organization in new directions — being unsatisfied with maintaining the status quo.	Concentrate on maximizing results from existing functions and systems.
Communicate the purpose of doing things.	Communicate directives, policies and procedures.
Favor taking risks and making changes.	Fear uncertainty and act cautiously.
Generate a feeling of meaning in work — its value and importance.	Enforce fulfillment of agreements and contracts for work.

Every organization needs both leaders and managers. Leaders are needed to light the way to the future and to inspire people to achieve excellence. Managers are essential to ensure that day-to-day operations run smoothly and that the assets of the corporation, both human and physical, are cared for and protected.

Obviously, it is possible for a person to have both leadership and managerial skills, and various combinations are possible. My observation, however, has been that every executive tends to favor one or the other, not both.

According to Harold Geneen, who led the International Telephone and Telegraph Company for seventeen years, "Leadership is the single most important ingredient in business management. Eighty to ninety percent of an organization's success is dependent on the leadership attributes of the manager to inspire his or her people to excel."[5]

The primary motivation to become a leader should be the inner satisfaction that comes from giving of yourself to create, mold and nuture competence in a work group or organization. The size of the accomplishment is not what is important. Rather it is the creation of something of worth or value in this world. It could be as small as being a mentor for a promising young manager or as large as turning around an unprofitable company. On the other hand, when the quest for wealth, status or the acclaim of others supersedes the inner satisfaction motive, a failure of leadership inevitably follows.

As a leader you are invested with special trust and competence to produce excellence in your organization and to ensure equity and fair treatment for all personnel. Success in this dual role does not come easily but requires considerable investment in time and energy.

Being a leader has its advantages in terms of recognition, prestige and status. Other benefits such as higher pay and special perks are important, too. Possibly the greatest reward is the feeling of self-worth that comes from being able to directly influence the course of events of an important enterprise. With this power comes the responsibility for followers and the responsibility to achieve the goals of the organization.

The responsibility for others — in terms of their welfare, morale, and development — cannot be overemphasized. Con-

The role of the leader is to shepherd the operation so that the selfish goals of the individual managers blend to support the goals of the firm.

> *Richard S. Sloma*
> *Chairman,*
> *Sigma Group*

The price of greatness is responsibility.

> *Winston*
> *Churchill*

7

sider that most employees spend more than one-half of their waking hours under the influence and direction of their leaders at work. What an opportunity for leaders to have a positive influence in this world!

Leading others is not always easy. Certain hardships go with the benefits. First, there is the constant strain and tension of having to produce results and to be at your best. You cannot afford to let down and relax.

Prior to becoming a leader, when you were only a member of the group, you had more security. If the group did not perform well, it was not all your fault — you shared the blame with others. As a leader you cannot hide in the crowd. You are directly responsible and accountable for the results of your personnel.

Being a successful leader requires personal sacrifices.

Second, long hours are required of leaders both on and off the job. Eleven and twelve hour days are often the norm in addition to being constantly on-call after hours.

Finally, being a leader means that you are no longer one of the gang and cannot maintain the same relationships with the group members that you once enjoyed. When placed in charge, you are expected to be able to say "no," administer discipline and make decisions that may not be well received by some people. You face the risk of being rejected by your old friends, frequently second-guessed and talked about behind your back.

It **is** lonely at the top! If this bothers you, leading people may not be your cup of tea.

Is it all worth it? That depends on your personality and desires in life. Each individual must make his or her own decision about being a leader by weighing the pros and cons. To me, it is all worth it and more!

II

The Challenge of Leadership

The typical business leader's world is unique since it is composed of a number of diverse special interest groups each with their own sets of needs, expectations and priorities (see illustration below). The leader is responsible for integrating and coordinating the functions and activities of the various groups as well as energizing each individual to do the best job possible. What makes this role such a challenge is that the leader has limited authority and control over the people with whom he interacts. Success in meeting the goals of the organization is dependent

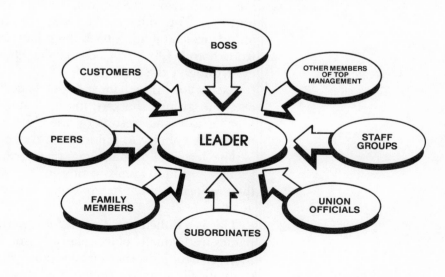

upon his ability to secure the commitment and cooperation of everyone involved. The leader cannot dictate, order or will that this be done. He must persuade and inspire others to **willingly** cooperate.

Leadership in this respect can be likened to the role of a catalyst, an agent that causes a chemical reaction when mixed with another compound. Nothing happens until the catalyst is introduced. Another analogy is that of an accomplished orchestra conductor who draws out the best efforts of his musicians to create a beautiful symphony. Without the conductor the musicians' efforts would be flat and disjointed.

Obtaining commitment to a common mission from the groups that interact with the leader is difficult because many of them inherently want different things. For example, upper-management typically insists that the leader take strong measures to improve productivity. Subordinates, feeling overworked already, would rather be left alone to focus on finding ways to make their jobs more varied and interesting. Improving productivity only for the benefit of the company turns them off.

Staff groups (i.e., Personnel, Industrial Engineering, Quality Control and Safety) want the leader to give top priority to their pet projects or programs. The leader's spouse and children also have their own expectations, such as wanting more family time together. This may conflict with the leader's ambition to get ahead, which often requires long hours and frequent travel away from home. Obviously, the leader cannot give top priority to everything at the same time.

Except for immediate staff the leader has no formal authority over the groups that are instrumental in determining success. Unable to obtain results by merely issuing directives, he must rely on the ability to influence and persuade.

The leadership challenge, therefore, is to convince various groups and individuals to buy-in to a set of common goals and then to inspire them to work together as a team to achieve these goals.

This is a difficult task, even for experienced leaders. Yet, companies traditionally place relatively untrained people in first-level management jobs, the very positions where sound leadership can dramatically improve quality and productivity.

The need for effective leaders at all levels of business and public service has never been so great.

The problem of inadequate leadership at the lower levels of management has its roots in our educational system. High schools and colleges do not emphasize leadership skills in the required curriculum. In addition, young people today prefer to make money working after school as short-order cooks or clerks rather than developing their leadership skills in extracurricular activities. They learn to take orders, not give them. The result is that most young people entering the work force do not have an understanding of how to lead others.

In the work place the situation is not much better since most companies do not offer premanagement programs to prepare candidates for advancement. When promoted, the untrained individual is suddenly expected to effectively lead fifteen to twenty subordinates in the complex social environment previously described. No wonder that the leadership failure rate is so high at the first and second levels of management.

Typically, the first-level managers are selected for their traits of being hard-working, conscientious and assertive. Once promoted they usually set out to make their mark by quickly improving performance deficiencies. They often forget about the vital necessity of first gaining the loyalty and support of subordinates before making major changes.

As with most newly appointed managers, this happened to me when I joined Sealtest Foods at age twenty-two. After a short stint selling, I was given the job of managing a trucking operation in northern Virginia. This branch had the worst performance record in the Eastern Region. Overtime was excessive, productivity was low and sales volume was behind forecast. I was determined to shape things up in a hurry. Besides trying to move too quickly, I made the mistake of not involving the truck drivers in restructuring their delivery routes. As employee resentment grew, I reacted by pressing company policies even harder.

One morning when I arrived at 6:00 a.m. to observe the sort and load operation, I found the drivers milling around and talking instead of working. They decided that they had enough of my by-the-book approach and wanted to talk to the local union president and to my boss Bill Wade. Bill, who had been a union official himself and had good rapport with the men, persuaded them to resume work while he became involved in the issues.

That evening, and well into the night, Bill counseled me until I realized that I was applying too much pressure on the men to obtain immediate results. My reaction to this insight was to let up, to be the "good guy." This, too, led nowhere. Overtime remained high and productivity low. It was not until about the seventh month on the job that I began to slowly provide the proper mix of challenging the drivers to excell and being concerned about their welfare. After a year and a half the branch became the most profitable in the region, winning an award for excellence.

There is an important lesson to be learned from this experience: **the loyalty and support of subordinates must be obtained before the leader attempts to implement his or her vision of the future.** This requires that the leader be patient and successfully apply the principles of effective leadership described in the following chapters.

III

The Development of Leadership Style

Before building a profile of an effective leader, I need to emphasize one point. Leaders are **made,** not born. The "born leader" school believes that a leader's style is determined by his or her genetic inheritance. The opposing viewpoint, to which I subscribe, is that leadership style is acquired in the same manner as are sophistication and graciousness — by study, emulation and experience.

From years of participating in the development of managers, I know it is possible for individuals to shape and change their behavior so as to be more successful in inspiring and energizing others. This requires understanding one's limitations and desiring to overcome them.

Dwight Eisenhower was a leader who was made, not born. During World War I, when many of Eisenhower's West Point classmates were fighting and earning medals in Europe, he was stagnating in a Pentagon desk job. Shortly after the war, Eisenhower requested a transfer to Panama to work under General Fox Conner, a senior officer whom he admired. In a highly charged situation Eisenhower was tutored by his mentor in every aspect of military leadership. As Eisenhower later wrote about Conner:

> Life with General Connor was sort of a graduate school in military affairs and the humanities, leavened by a man who was experienced in his knowledge of men and their conduct. I can never adequately express

my gratitude to this one gentleman . . . In a lifetime of association with great and good men, he is the one, more or less, invisible figure to whom I owe an incalculable debt.[1]

With the basic premise that leadership skills are nurtured and developed during one's lifetime, let us now turn our attention to learning what effective leaders do that is worth emulating.

IV

Profile of An Effective Leader

The Central Engine Repair Shop of a major international airline was considered a managerial graveyard. Over the years a number of managers had failed to lift the shop's low productivity. With each organizational change the mechanics continued to do what they pleased — reading newspapers and magazines at their work stations, taking twenty-five minute coffee breaks, and regularly washing up one-half hour before quitting time. Efforts to eliminate such practices were met with slow-downs and sick-outs.

The Vice-President of Maintenance and Engineering had almost accepted this condition as a way of life when Ed Martin, an experienced, respected manager from another department, requested to be transferred to the position. When asked why he did so, he replied, ''I just have a feeling that deep down, most of the guys aren't happy about the shop's poor reputation. I think I can make them feel like winners.''

The first thing Ed did was to hold a meeting with the shop stewards in his office. Instead of sitting behind his desk as was customary, Ed asked them to join him at a round conference table. For several hours they talked about the problems and opportunities in the engine shop. Nothing was decided that day, but one of the union officials was later overheard as saying, ''I can't believe how he treated us as equals — no big-boss attitude, that's for sure.'' At one of the subsequent meetings a safety problem was identified that had been allowed to continue for nearly a year. In a few days Ed had the problem corrected. By continuing the dialogue and by taking strong action to resolve a number of small but potentially explosive issues, the mechanics began to gain confidence in Ed. Everyone did not agree with what was done, but there was a growing feeling in the shop that the new boss was fair and could make things happen. Next, Ed established several committees to develop suggestions for improving quality and safety. He even got a group involved in planning a baseball tournament and family cookout.

The difficult issue of adhering to break and quitting times was handled by explaining to everyone how the low productivity made it difficult to win competitive bids on outside engine contract work. Additional overtime for those who wanted it would be lost by not getting the business. By the time Ed put the word out that the rules and regulations would be enforced, many of the mechanics had already changed their ways. Those that did not were firmly handled on an individual basis.

By the end of Ed's first year on the job the Engine Shop's productivity and quality levels were among the best of all shops in the Maintenance and Engineering Division. Ed knew the battle was won when he arrived one morning to find a huge banner strung across the hanger wall. It read: "We're #1."

Ulysses S. Grant faced a similar but much broader problem than Ed Martin when Abraham Lincoln promoted him to Lieutenant General of all Northern armies in early 1864. Except for the battle of Gettysburg the Union had suffered decisive defeats at the hands of Robert E. Lee at Bull Run (1861 and 1862), Fredericksburg and Chancellorsville. Grant's army was riddled with green draftees. Morale was poor due to inadequate leadership. In many units proper provisions were lacking.

At first, some of the troops were uncertain if the new general's name was Ulysses or Useless.[1] Then, conditions slowly began to change. Equipment formerly lacking materialized suddenly. Infantry units that had spent the war in easy jobs defending Washington, D.C., were reassigned to the front. The cavalry, which had previously been encumbered with endless picket details, assumed an exciting new role. Now they were deployed as compact hit-and-run strike forces. A perceptible tightening-up occurred when officers began to monitor even routine jobs.

Artillery units were drilled hour after hour until they achieved perfection in their maneuvers. The new spirit under Grant was best expressed by a New England trooper in one of his letters to home: "We all felt at last that the **boss** had arrived."[2]

The September 9, 1985, edition of the *Wall Street Journal* carried an interesting story of two top steel executives with radically different leadership styles. It was reported that several thousand striking workers of the Wheeling-Pittsburgh Steel Corporation gathered outside the Steubenville, Ohio, plant to symbolically lynch company chairman Dennis J. Carney. A straw effigy of the chairman was raised to the top of a lamppost and later lowered and burned. Even before the strike began, the Wheeling Company had sought and obtained protection under the bankruptcy laws.

According to the *Journal,* Mr. Carney had ruled the company with an iron hand for nearly five years. The article cited the example of Mr. Carney's visit to the Monessen, Pennsylvania, plant in 1982. Instead of greeting and mixing with employees he called a private session with a group of hourly and salaried workers. "He then proceeded to launch into what was described as a tirade. 'He practically accused us of conspiring to sabotage his mill,' recalls David Kissler, one of the workers who attended the meeting. Such outbursts, whether on the shop floor or in the corporate suite, are typical of what former employees contended was Mr. Carney's management by intimidation style."[3]

The *Journal* then described what happened directly across the Ohio River from the Wheeling-Pittsburgh plant in another steel company — the Weirton Steel Corporation. Mr. Robert L. Loughhead, who headed Weirton, was considered to be a very effective leader. Mr. Loughhead spent considerable time in the plant observing operations and talking to employees. "There's only so much he can do," said steelworker Frank Loggie, "but just the fact that he's there shows you he cares."[4] The affable chairman was a consensus-style executive who went out of his way to involve all levels in policy decisions. He encouraged open and honest communications up and down the line. The results speak for themselves — Weirton is the nation's most profitable steelmaker.

The highest compliment a leader can receive is one that is given by the people who work for him.

23

Successful leaders, such as Ed Martin, Ulysses Grant and Robert Loughhead act in a way that elicits the support and following of others. These qualities of leadership will be as important in the next century as they were in the past.

At one point in my career I thought that charisma was necessary to lead others successfully. I have since learned that charisma is helpful, but not necessary to achieve excellent results through others. Many effective leaders that I have observed seem to have little popular appeal. Their lack of charisma is usually offset by other leadership qualities, such as those presented in this book.

It should be emphasized that real skill in leading others has to be natural and sincere. "Techniques" contrived to manipulate people will not work. Your employees have the uncanny ability to judge the true you by your actions and deeds.

There are seventeen basic leadership attributes or qualities that are important in leading others. Together they present a profile of a leader who has compassion and consideration for his or her personnel while at the same time holding them strictly accountable for results. Some industrial psychologists call this "tough love." The profile also includes desired personal traits of the leader, such as integrity, honesty and morality in addition to the intangible factors of determination and courage.

There is no simple formula for leadership success. Nor is it possible to reach perfection in each leadership skill. Also, the capacity to lead gradually builds over time. However, **one's leadership development can be accelerated by constantly visualizing the ideal leadership attributes and modeling one's own behavior after them.** These leadership attributes or qualities are presented in the next seventeen chapters. From this material you will be exposed to numerous ideas and models that will help you improve your leadership performance.

1

The Effective Leader Builds Group Cohesiveness and Pride

Deep within all of us is the desire to be a winner—to be somebody.

The fuel that runs all successful organizations is the pride and sense of accomplishment that comes from striving for and achieving high levels of performance. Employees want to be a part of a winning team. Successful teamwork is exciting, upbeat and offers personal rewards such as status, recognition and, in many cases, additional renumeration.

At the close of the 1984 football season Raymond Berry was hired to be interim coach of the New England Patriots, a team that had never played in a title game. In just one season the Patriots were transformed into the champions of the American Football Conference. Tackle Bryan Holloway was asked how Berry did it. His response: "Berry showed us how to win. It's like the old saying: If you give a man a fish, you feed him for a day. But if you show him how to catch fish, you feed him for life . . . He made us believe we were the better team, and that belief can unleash awesome power when you take it out on the field with you."[1]

In October 1981, Pete Willmott, President of Federal Express, made a visit to the Philadelphia Airport Station. He was appalled by the trash and dirt on the warehouse floor, noticed a stack of brooms, picked up one and began sweeping. The employees were so shocked that soon they were doing the same thing. Pete had made the employees aware of their lack of **pride** and attention to detail. The sloppy warehouse was indicative of the station's performance in other areas. Overtime was excessive, and the aircraft were seldom loaded on time.

Well led followers feel useful, important and part of a worthwhile enterprise.

Shortly after Mr. Willmott's visit Tennyson Lewis was transferred to the Philadelphia position. It didn't take long for Tennyson to realize that the cargo handlers were dissatisfied with present conditions. Most of them felt that there was little direction and organization.

Tennyson spent the first few months getting to know the employees and learning the operation. Slowly, he began to plant the seed that the Philadelphia Station could become the best in the system. This vision was a long way from the prevailing viewpoint in the company that Philadelphia was almost a lost cause.

It was not long until Tennyson's supervisors and several respected handlers began supporting the idea of going for it—making a major performance turnaround. The thought of redeeming themselves for the sweeping incident became appealing. Pride in performance was now a part of the group's goals.

With hope for an improved future the Philadelphia management team began making improvements everywhere. Briefings were initiated prior to each shift to review work assignments and to provide updates on what was happening in other parts of the company. New training programs began. Badly needed equipment was secured, and the office and warehouse were painted. Most importantly, management encouraged everyone to give his best and recognized each person when good work was performed.

When I visited the station a year later, the change was remarkable. The ramp crew had loaded and fueled two hundred and fifty consecutive flights without delay. Not only did the Philadelphia crew take great pride in this unusual accomplishment, but they also made sure I got a tour of their "new" facility: the same building, but with a fresh, clean look everywhere. You could have eaten off the floor!

Like Raymond Berry and Tennyson Lewis, high performing leaders do two key things to build group cohesiveness and pride. First and foremost, they **establish and articulate visions of what could be for their organizations.** Often these visions take the shape of "heroic goals" — possible levels of performance or achievement of such scope or magnitude that, if achieved, substantially enhance the status and prestige of the organizations.

Everyone likes to be a part of a winning team, especially if the team is a **big** winner. Going after the heroic goal or the ultimate

Compare yourself to the world's best performers in your industry, then set goals that exceed the best.

Tom Peters

level of performance creates a common mission with which everyone can identify. In baseball the ultimate achievement is winning the World Series. In horse racing it is winning the Triple Crown. Examples of heroic goals in the business world are obtaining the highest level of profitability in the *Fortune* 500, operating with the best level of quality in the plant or the lowest accident rate in the company.

The greater the obstacle, the more glory in overcoming it.

Molière

The role of the leader is to identify challenging overall objectives and to interest the organization in going after them. Edwin H. Land, founder of the Polaroid Corporation, had the right idea when he said, "The first thing you naturally do is teach the person to feel that the undertaking is manifestly important and nearly impossible."[2]

The importance of creating a feeling of ownership of the heroic goal cannot be overstated. It is one thing to identify a challenging goal and quite another to get people excited about going after it. If the manager tries to force the goal on his people, they will resist. Forcing change of any type makes employees feel like serfs in a feudal management kingdom — victims of management's whims. This natural feeling of resentment may not be visually apparent, but it simmers beneath the surface. Under such conditions employees go through the motions of doing the new job or task, but their hearts and souls are not in it.

How different it is when employees are **involved** in the planning stages of change and can create their own strategies for reaching the heroic goals. When someone owns something, he takes better care of it. Just ask yourself: When was the last time I waxed a rental car?

Once the heroic goal is identified, a good leader promotes it extensively. This important step is often neglected. **One of the secrets of effective leadership is to promote employee communications and motivational programs with the same intensity as marketing to customers.**

The best way to create employee awareness of a heroic goal is through symbols and slogans. To be effective they must be unusual and catchy. Two of the most successful internal advertising campaigns that I have used to promote heroic goals featured a bull dog and a sloppily dressed businessman (see next page).

The $40M Challenge. Federal Express field operating personnel were asked to be "bull dog tough" in reducing costs by $40 million during a six month period. Posters and banners featuring a bulldog were used to introduce the campaign. To consistently stress the theme, weekly newsletters were published detailing individual and group cost saving successes. Routine correspondence was stamped with impressions similar to the above.

The Enemy Of Excellence...

A two phase program to substantially improve service levels. First, pictures of Mr. Good Enough (created by Ft. Myers courier Lynn Blily) were distributed to field managers with a memo describing the philosophy that being good enough to have the best on-time delivery service in the industry was no longer acceptable. Only 100% achievement would be satisfactory from then on. Next, a Circle of Excellence Award Program was announced. Stations that achieved exceptional service levels were featured in the company newspaper and group pictures of their personnel were displayed in a glass enclosed frame located at the corporate headquarters.

Even the best promotional efforts are of no avail unless you, the leader, continually stress goal achievement in day-to-day activities. Be enthusiastic about possibilities for improvement. Encourage creative thinking. Look for signs of progress, no matter how small. Celebrate successes. Thank those who make an extra effort. Place a premium on teamwork. You need to do all these things and much more.

In time people will respond to your constant encouragement and enthusiasm. Before long you will be looking for another heroic goal that is more challenging than the first.

Progress results from not being satisfied.

Frank Tyger

Tennyson Lewis, the Philadelphia Station Manager, did not stop when his crew achieved 250 days without an aircraft delay. When it appeared that they would go a full year without a delay, he convinced everyone that two years would be a target worthy of even more distinction. The idea is to never be satisfied. Keep raising the sights of the organization.

People working in cooperative ventures need to be constantly energized by undertaking new challenges; they need to climb new mountains. You want your personnel to be stimulated so as to release their energy and creativity — or, in other words, to contribute at their capacity.

A word of caution about establishing heroic goals. Be careful not to overwhelm subordinates by expecting too much too quickly. No one can work continuously at something without achieving some success. Good leaders break down the goal into small, obtainable pieces. The idea is to slowly build everyone's confidence — to develop the attitude of being a winner. After a few successes the group will be ready to take on the big challenge.

The second step effective leaders take to build group cohesiveness and pride is to **provide abundant feedback and recognition.** The need for frequent feedback is best illustrated by asking: How long would you continue playing tennis or golf if you couldn't keep score? Not very long. In the game of business, people need the same constant stream of information on how they are doing.

What gets rewarded, gets done.

As soon as group or team performance data is available, put it on charts and graphs for everyone to see. Small improvements should be noted and encouragement offered. When good work is turned in or an extra effort made, give compliments. People thrive on praise, and the natural reaction to receiving it is to try

People are not motivated by failure; they are motivated by achievement and recognition.

F. F. Fournies, **Coaching for Improved Work Performance**

Outstanding leaders go out of their way to boost the self-esteem of their personnel. It is the key to performance improvement.

even harder. The leader's enthusiasm for what has been accomplished is infectious. There will be a feeling of pride in meeting tough standards or goals.

One of the best ways to recognize the outstanding performance of an individual or team is to do it in front of others. Make it a practice never to conduct a staff meeting without some form of planned recognition. Lavish praise on outstanding performers and, when appropriate, present them with a tangible award such as a gift certificate, plaque or letter of commendation.

Federal Express does this with their Bravo-Zulo Award Program. Bravo-Zulu, a Navy term that stands for a job well done, is depicted by two large flags that are flown on ship masts to recognize excellence. A manager at Federal has the ability to make Bravo-Zulo awards on the spot by giving an individual a small set of flags and a check ranging from $50 to $100.

Years ago I was involved in an incident that dramatically illustrates the power of simple recognition as a motivator. While serving as Station Manager at Newark Airport for Eastern Airlines, I sent a letter of commendation to a burly ramp serviceman to recognize his outstanding leadership in directing the unloading of a leaking package of dangerous chemicals. Had he not acted quickly and decisively, there could have been a serious aircraft fire. About two weeks after he received the letter, he approached me and said in his usually gruff manner, ''Mr. Manske, do you know what I did with your letter?'' I expected the worst, but he said, ''I put it on the door of my refrigerator at home.'' The ramp serviceman was so proud of being recognized that he posted the letter in **the** place in American homes reserved for truly important items. I had no idea that a simple letter of recognition could mean so much.

A word of praise is far more meaningful to a person if it is related to one of his or her **qualities** (such as leadership ability, positive attitude or honesty) than if it is tied to performance results. People like to be appreciated for their inner qualities first and then for what they produce. For example, instead of saying, ''Good job on getting the XYZ account,'' try something more personal, such as, ''I admire your determination to keep working on the XYZ account until you got the business.'' This approach means that you have to become familiar with the abilities and performance of each of your employees, but it is well worth the extra effort.

Praise can be a powerful motivator **if** it is a sincere expression on the part of the boss and **if** it is related to specific, well-deserved performance accomplishments. Have you ever had a boss lavish praise on you when it was not deserved? Or, have you ever been complimented on a job when you have not even finished it? How did you feel? Not very good, I suspect. People resent receiving a pat on the back or a note saying, "Good job, keep it up," from a manager who has only a vague idea of what they do. The lesson here is obvious. Limit your praise to situations where it is deserved and where you know precisely what improvement was made.

The leader must also be careful to give credit and recognition unselfishly to those that deserve it. Don Shula, head coach of the Miami Dolphins (two-time Super Bowl champions) does this whenever he appears on television or at a community fund raising dinner. He always gives his team credit for his success. Rather than "I did it," Shula says, "They did it," or, "We did it."

In summary, to build the group cohesiveness and pride that is necessary for outstanding performance, the leader must do two essential things:

1. Establish and articulate a vision of what **could be** for the organization (i.e., establish a heroic goal); and
2. Provide abundant feedback, recognition and appreciation.

There is no limit to what a man can do or where he can go if he doesn't mind who gets the credit.

Author Unknown

2

The Effective Leader Lives By The Highest Standards of Honesty and Integrity

An honest man is the noblest work of God.

Alexander Pope

In the book *Profiles of Leadership* America's top business and government leaders were asked what quality they thought was most important to their success as a leader. Their unanimous answer: **integrity**. A similar result was obtained in an American Management Association sponsored survey of 1500 managers.[1]

Dwight D. Eisenhower had these words to say about the importance of integrity:

> In order to be a leader a man must have followers. And to have followers, a man must have their confidence. Hence the supreme quality for a leader is unquestionably integrity. Without it, no real success is possible, no matter whether it is on a section gang, a football field, in an army, or in an office. If a man's associates find him guilty of phoniness, if they find that he lacks forthright integrity, he will fail. His teachings and action must square with each other. The first great need therefore, is integrity and high purpose.[2]

It is one thing to **talk** about integrity and honesty, and it is quite another to **live** your life that way. The true test of honesty is a truthful answer to this question: Would you return money that was given to you in error (say, by a bank teller or store cashier) when you knew you had the opportunity to keep it without being caught?

Honesty and integrity are best taught by example.

Recently at a large retailing company, thirty-five senior executives were given a paper and pencil honesty test. Prior to the test, they were guaranteed absolute anonymity. The results: two-thirds of the executives admitted that they occasionally falsified their expense accounts.[3]

In just one recent year three *Fortune* 500 companies pleaded guilty to crimes ranging from fraud to issue of false claims for government contract expenses. In addition, the chairmen of the board of two large industrial firms, a bank president and a defense contractor were sentenced to jail terms for misuse of company funds and obstruction of justice. Only a few months after these scandals Wall Street was rocked with the arrest of several high level officials from the leading stock brokerage firms for alleged insider trading abuses. These disturbing incidences of high-level leaders acting as if they were above the law present poor examples for those aspiring to reach the top.

Corruption and dishonesty seem to occur when the leader loses sight of the fact that he or she is given power for **one** purpose — to serve others. Harry Truman put it another way: "If a man can accept a situation in a place of power with the thought that it's only temporary, he comes out all right. But when he thinks he is the **cause** of the power, that can be his ruination."

W. F. Smith, a noted Dallas businessman, goes a step further with his concept of power. He says that "power for good flows through you from God. It does not originate with you." In other words you are not the source of power, but a conduit through which it flows. Maintaining one's humility should never be a problem for a leader if he or she keeps Mr. Smith's viewpoint in mind.

Besides maintaining a proper perspective about their power, leaders must be careful not to place too much pressure on their personnel to achieve unrealistic goals. When subordinates realize that the only way to make targets is to cut corners, the seeds for unethical behavior are sown. Some employees who are unable to cope with the consequences of failure grasp at anything to retain their good standing in the organization — such as falsifying reports and purposely violating government regulations.

More than anything else, followers want to believe that their leaders are ethical and honest. They want to say, "Someday I want to be like him or her."

A good name is seldom regained. When character is gone, one of the richest jewels of life is lost forever.

J. Hanes

The greatest contribution leaders can make to mankind is to use their power in a positive way — to help and inspire others.

The development of highly-principled leaders is vitally important to the future of any organizaton. In a broader sense it is imperative for the future of our country. This is why I always close my leadership seminars or speeches with the following exhortation:

> If you would remember only one thing from this presentation let it be: live your life by the highest standards of honesty and integrity. Throughout your career you will be tempted to do the expedient, to shade the truth or violate moral principles. Stand firm, don't waiver, and someday you can look back at your accomplishments with pride and satisfaction, for you will have succeeded by doing things the right way without violating the trust given to you by your followers. More than anything else, your legacy will be that you inspired others to live their lives in a similar fashion.

Integrity in a leader must be **demonstrated** daily and in a number of tangible ways:

1. **Do what you say you will do.** If you promise something to a subordinate, colleague or superior, keep your word. Never hint at a possible future award to sugarcoat an unpleasant decision.

   Recently, the Center for Creative Leadership in Greensboro, North Carolina, released a study of twenty-one high potential executives who were terminated or forced to retire early from their companies. The one universal character flaw or unforgivable sin which always led to downfall was betraying a trust — not doing something that was promised.[4]

2. **Never divulge information given in confidence to you** by superiors or colleagues.

3. **Accept responsibility for your mistakes.** Every successful executive has made his or her share of mistakes. The trouble is that most people will not own up to them. Do not be afraid to say, "I made a mistake."

   The other day one of my associates missed an important

Integrity is not a given in everyone's life. It is the result of self-discipline, inner trust and a decision to be relentlessly honest in all situations in our lives.

*Workman
1987
Page-A-Day
Calendar*

meeting. When I asked him about it, he startled me by saying, "I just forgot." No other excuses were offered. My first thought was, "How refreshing."

Harold Geneen, past president of ITT, admitted in his book *Managing* that he made his share of mistakes at ITT. They did not ruin him because he was not adverse to accepting the blame for poor decisions.

Every time people engage in dishonest or immoral acts, the results come back to haunt them.

4. **Never become involved in a falsehood or a lie.** If your employees ever catch you misrepresenting the facts, lying to them or covering up a problem, you will lose credibility instantly. And it will not be easy to regain.

Dr. William Schultz, a noted psychologist who developed truth-in-management strategies at Proctor and Gamble and NASA, believes the key to productivity is "how well people work together and that nothing increases compatibility like mutual trust and honesty."[5] He continues by saying, "If people in business just told the truth, 80 to 90% of their problems would disappear."[6] Trust and honesty then become the means that allow individuals to cooperate so that they can all prosper.

5. **Avoid accepting gifts or gratuities from inside or outside the company that compromise your ability to perform in the best interest of your employer.** This is an area where I have seen a number of capable young managers go astray. Problems usually begin when they accept a small gift from a supplier at Christmas. Soon they are being entertained at a lavish resort for a weekend. It is not hard to imagine what happens after that.

Maintaining high standards of honesty and integrity in today's business world takes an inner toughness and resolve to persevere, often under extreme pressure or even under the threat of losing your job. Situations may arise when superiors expect you to do something unethical or dishonest. It may be an order to keep quiet about a safety flaw in a product, a demand to alter financial statements or a request not to report a plant accident. Torn between upholding your values and loyalty to superiors, you must make a choice. You can compromise yourself by doing the expedient, or you can stand up for what you believe and take the consequences. In the long run you are better off to do what is

The key question you must always ask yourself: "What is the right thing to do?"

right. Having a free conscience is important to being able to live with yourself. One can take great pride in saying, "I made it without cheating or abusing others." Also, ethical business leaders are in demand in the vast majority of companies. Therefore, do not waste valuable career time in organizations that do not revere high values.

There is no pillow as soft as a clear conscience.
John Wooden

The true measure of living your life by the highest standards of honesty and integrity comes if you can go any place in the world and never encounter someone who can point a finger at you and say, "That man did me in."

Remember, **without integrity you do not have trust, and without trust you have nothing!**

The Three-Way Test To Determine
If A Decision Or Action Is Ethical

I DOES IT VIOLATE ANY LAWS OR COMPANY POLICIES?[7]

II IS IT FAIR TO ALL CONCERNED?[8]

III AM I PROUD OF IT; PROUD ENOUGH TO TELL MY FAMILY AND FRIENDS ABOUT IT?[9]

For a decision or action to be considered ethical, the answer to question number one should be ''no'' and the answers to questions two and three should be ''yes.'' A different answer to any of the questions should serve as a red light; stop and reconsider your decision or plan of attack.

3

The Effective Leader Shares Information Openly and Willingly

From years of talking to employees throughout the world I find they all share the common desire to be "in on stuff." They want to be taken into confidence about where their company is headed and how future plans might affect them. Clear answers must be provided to "what's in it for me" questions, such as what will be gained in terms of status, pay, working conditions and job satisfaction.

It is not important that everyone understands all the details of the company's strategies. A general understanding will do. The point is that by taking the time to share information, the leader demonstrates that he or she values the individual as an important member of the organization.

Sharing information about goals and strategies is very important to the success of an organization. People need to know where they are headed before they can make commitments to place group needs above their own.

What employees **do not** want is a lot of formal corporate communications, such as newspapers or letters from top management. These forms of communications tend to be impersonal and rarely address the real issues on the front line. Everyone wants the straight scoop without all of the embellishments and carefully chosen words that typify most communications from headquarters. What is most desired is **frequent, candid information** from the immediate boss.

When I was the Newark Airport Station Manager for Eastern Airlines in the late 1970's, I had a very capable ramp manager named Tom Chuchran. Tom had a difficult job in that he was responsible for motivating several hundred ramp servicemen who loaded and unloaded passenger luggage all day. Because of the repetitious nature of the work, there was a tendency to be lackadaisical in sorting bags to the proper connecting flights. To complicate matters, Tom's personnel were represented by a strong union.

For several years I had the opportunity to observe first-hand Tom's exceptional style of personal communications. Tom spent most of the day talking to his men one-on-one or in small groups. He once told me that he made it a point to see all of his team at least once a day. This was not an easy task since the operation ran from 6:00 a.m. until midnight.

More than anything else, Tom was sincerely interested in the welfare of each person. He made it a point to keep track of employee illnesses and serious personal problems. If an individual was sick in the hospital, Tom went out of his way to visit him. On more than one occasion he loaned money to a person with a serious financial problem.

Tom always seemed to be available to answer questions about the operation or to lend a hand when needed. When each shift punched in, he was present in the ready room. At break time he often could be seen drinking coffee with his men. Even at the end of the day Tom was available to anyone who wanted to talk. Often he accompanied one or two employees to their cars after work.

The Newark employees viewed Tom as a trusted source of information about the company. If a question was raised that he could not answer, he would admit that he did not know, but would find out. I do not recall Tom ever failing to keep such a promise. Around the airport it was said that if you wanted to get the straight scoop, just ask Tom.

Let us examine Tom's communication style to see why it was so effective. Foremost, he was in constant touch with his personnel, sharing and disseminating information. Tom instinctively knew that the major reason for poor communications is the **assumption** that everyone understands what to do and why. He therefore went out of his way to carefully explain new directives

The basic building block of good communications is the feeling that every human being is unique and of value.

— especially the reasons and rationale for them. Information about future plans was readily given. For example, if discussions were being held at headquarters concerning possible flight increases or cutbacks at Newark, employees were kept appraised. No one therefore felt a need to develop a rumor mill. Disruptive rumors never had a chance to get off the ground.

Tom's ramp servicemen responded to the concern and attention shown them by being open and candid in return. They had ample opportunities to get things off their chests without resorting to more drastic measures. Such freedom of expression enabled Tom to clear up misunderstandings and minor irritations before they developed into formal grievances.

More than once, Tom Chuchran's intimate style of communication saved the day for Eastern at Newark Airport. On one cold winter night the termination of an employee led to a slow down in baggage handling. Passengers were waiting two hours for their luggage. Only because of their respect and trust for Tom was everyone persuaded to resume their normal pace of work.

4

The Effective Leader Coaches To Improve Performance

It is only as we develop others that we permanently succeed.

Harvey S. Firestone

Create the kind of climate in your organization where personal growth is expected, recognized and rewarded.

The most important responsibility of a leader is to develop personnel. Your success as a leader is dependent upon how well your people perform. One of the major reasons managers are not promoted is that they do not have someone ready to replace them. It is therefore in your best interest to make employee development your number one priority.

The ultimate leader is one who is willing to develop personnel to the point that they eventually surpass him or her in knowledge and ability. This generative process is necessary for the long-term prosperity of the company.

There are two prerequisites for personal development to occur. First, there must be a supportive environment for learning. Second, the individual must want to learn.

In a supportive learning environment the leader-coach **encourages** employees to try new things and take calculated risks to improve performance. Personal growth will not occur unless experimentation is fostered. Under such conditions employees will make mistakes. The important element is how the leader reacts to them. If he accepts honest mistakes as the price for innovation, employees will not be afraid to keep seeking better ways of doing things. In such an environment the focus is always on what **can** be learned from the failure. In effect, mistakes become stepping stones to success.

One of the first jobs I had after graduating from college was purchasing trucks for Sealtest Foods. One day after spending considerable time reviewing bids for a sizable order of tractor trailers, I made a recommendation to the Director of Purchasing that we award the contract to Ford. After a verbal order was placed with Ford I discovered a mistake in my computations; another company offered more value for the same price. I will never forget the day I made my way to the director's office to inform him of my mistake. I can even recall the overcast sky that day and the dark green color of the rug in the elevator. After I nervously confessed my error, the director sat back in his chair and reflected for what seemed like an eternity. Finally, he said, "I'm disappointed in the quality of your work on this project, but all is not lost if you learned something." Rather than make me feel foolish and incompetent, he expressed confidence that I would be more thorough with the next bid.

This incident had a lasting impression on my life. I decided at that time that I would always make **quality**, not speed, the most important consideration in my work.

One evening I visited the Long Beach Station of Federal Express just as the couriers were returning from their routes. I watched with interest as the managers helped the couriers unload their trucks. While sharing the work tasks of the evening, the managers encouraged the couriers to talk about the good and the bad events of the day. What a beautiful way to demonstrate empathy and concern, to learn about the problems encountered and to make suggestions on how to improve performance!

The second prerequisite for personal development to occur is that the individual must want to improve his knowledge and skills. The drive to learn can only come from within the person. No one can force an individual to pay attention and absorb new material.

The leader-coach can influence this drive by the example he sets in his own developmental practices and by his belief in the trainee's capacity for growth. If someone believes in you, it is a powerful incentive for you to live up to that belief. A story from my youth illustrates this important point. After my junior high school graduation my homeroom teacher came up to me to offer her congratulations. Her parting words went something like this: "Fred, you've had a great year, and all the teachers including myself are proud of your accomplishments. We know you'll do

If your subordinates aren't making an occasional mistake or two, it's a sure sign they're playing it too safe.

Those who believe in our ability do more than stimulate us. They create for us an atmosphere in which it becomes easier to succeed.

John H. Spalding

well in senior high.'' With such an expression of confidence in me, how could I do anything but try my best in the future?

With a supportive environment for learning firmly established in the organization and a willingness to learn on the individual's part, it is now up to the leader-coach to guide and facilitate employee performance improvement by (1) asking the proper questions, (2) encouraging and reinforcing behavioral change and (3) providing an example of excellence for others to follow.

The role of the coach is to teach his players to stand on their own feet.

Good coaches know that real learning does not occur unless people are challenged to do their own thinking — to come up with their own ideas and solutions to problems without being given the answers.

The best way to stimulate such growth in your subordinates is to ask them open-ended questions that require thoughtful responses. Here are a few samples. I am sure you can think of many more.

- What are your recommendations?
- What do you think?
- Could the job be done a better way?
- What's not quite right in your operation?
- What are you planning to do?
- What do you want to accomplish during the next six months?

Encourage your personnel to explore new options instead of settling for the obvious.

Notice that none of these questions elicits a defensive reaction. Neither do they make the person feel dependent on the coach for his knowledge and expertise. Rather, they focus the discussion on the employee's thoughts and ideas, thereby developing his ability to think and make decisions. Contrast this developmental approach with one that is authoritative as illustrated by the boss saying, ''Your overtime is out of control; start cutting hours immediately!'' or ''The solution to your absenteeism problem is to give warning letters to the worst offenders.''

How different it is when the employees come up with their own solutions. Their commitment and the intensity of their action will be far stronger when such employee ownership exists than if they merely carry out the boss's precise directives. This does not mean that the boss should not coax or lead the employee in a certain direction. This is often necessary to avoid costly mistakes.

The use of the question, ''What do you want to accomplish during the next six months?'' is an excellent way for the leader to start an employee appraisal. It immediately focuses attention on the employee's plans for improving performance rather than dwelling on past failures and mistakes. Tension and defensiveness are minimized thereby opening minds for consideration of **what could be.** As the discussion of future possibilities continues, the employee will invariably identify his own deficiencies. It is at this point that the appraiser can add his own perspective by pointing out other areas that require improvement.

According to F.F. Fournies, writing in *Coaching For Improved Work Performance,* there are four common reasons why people do not perform the way they should:

1. They do not know **what** they are supposed to do.
2. They do not know **how** to do it.
3. They do not know **why** they should.
4. There are obstacles beyond their control.

Occasionally, there is a fifth reason for unsatisfactory performance: the person does not care enough to do the job properly. In other words, he has an attitude problem.

Fortunately, most people want to do a good job. When the leader asks the proper questions, he can quickly ascertain which areas of performance are deficient. Corrective action can then be taken by providing counseling or, if necessary, retraining.

If the employee has an attitude problem, you are faced with the difficult challenge of trying to change what the person cares about or what he believes. At this point the stakes are high, for if you cannot stimulate change for the better, you must discharge the individual.

People **can** adapt or change their attitudes if the inner motivation to do so is there. Acting as the catalyst for such change is one of the most difficult aspects of leadership. How does a leader facilitate positive changes in an individual's attitude and behavior?

Start by being frank and honest with the individual about how he is doing. Let him know what is good or bad. Honesty does not mean being brutal. It means indicating your displeasure about the performance deficiency in a firm, nonthreatening manner. For example, poor cost performance by a manager should be handled like this, "Ralph, your labor expenses continue to exceed budget by 8-10%. This is a serious problem that **must** be corrected. How do you plan to do it?"

Good leadership consists in showing average people how to do the work of superior people.

*John D.
Rockefeller*

Never criticize the personal qualities of the individual, such as his integrity, character or intelligence; criticize only the unsatisfactory quality of the work or the inappropriate action taken.

The hardest part of leadership is being candid with employees about performance deficiencies. Many managers fail miserably in this area because they wish to avoid conflict. Instead of dealing directly with the performance problems, they pass over them or treat them lightly in performance reviews. The result: No one wins. The employee does not receive the feedback that is necessary to improve, the boss does not get the excellence that is desired, and the company continues to be stuck with a marginal performer.

People prefer a leader who gives them the straight facts—good and bad.

Knowing where you stand with your boss is a universal need of every employee. This is best illustrated by the comments of a Federal Express manager in Florida, "The boss should tell you right away when you're doing wrong. A person wants to know this so he has an opportunity to correct the problem before it's too late."

Knowing where you stand with your boss is related to the basic human need for security. Your employees expect you to help them feel secure in their jobs; it is difficult to perform well when one expects a dismissal notice at any moment. Fearful employees are less productive in their jobs because they spend too much time and energy worrying about what their manager thinks about them. It is only when they feel secure that they can release their imaginations and creative energies.

Sell the advantages of cooperation and excellence.

After the leader-coach tells the employee how he feels about the peformance deficiency, it is important that the employee agree that there is a problem and realize that it is in his best interest to change for the better. Some people will react favorably if it is pointed out how their poor performance is adversely affecting the ability of co-workers to do their jobs or preventing the team from succeeding. Let the person know how others feel about having a weak link in the department. The implication is that if the offender will not improve, then the group may react by isolating him from social interaction.

Notice that I have shied away from referring to how the company will be affected by the individual's substandard work. Few people can identify with such an appeal because they see little

45

relationship between their performance and that of the entire company. However, they can empathize with how their associates might feel.

Normally, a frank performance discussion clears the air for both the leader and the employee. The leader has gotten an important matter off his chest that may have been bothering him for some time. The employee becomes aware of his shortcomings and has had an opportunity to express his viewpoints about them. He now realizes that his boss is displeased and expects improvement. The stage is now set for positive change.

After such performance counseling most people will make some effort, albeit small, to improve. Because even supportive feedback can make employees cautious, the initial improvement may hardly be noticeable. The employee is testing the water to see what happens. Here is a great opportunity for the leader-coach. If this initial effort to improve — as small as it may be — is noticed and recognized in a sincere way, the employee will try even harder the next time.

Giving encouragement to do even better can be a powerful stimulant for further improvement. Mary Kay Ash, founder and president of Mary Kay Cosmetics, uses this positive reinforcement approach with her employees. She says, "Forget their mistakes and zero in on one small thing they do right. Praise them and they'll do more things right and discover talents and abilities they never realized they had."[1]

The third way the leader-coach influences employee performance improvement is by setting an example. If the leader does not give his best, especially by demonstrating hard work and excellence, how can he expect subordinates to do the same?

When I was in the Coast Guard in the early 1960's, I served on two cutters. On the first ship the officers worked a minimal number of hours. They spent most of their time in the officers' mess reading magazines and drinking coffee. The crew responded in kind. We made a game of seeing how little work we could do without getting caught. Elaborate communication systems developed to signal the approach of an officer.

Our attitude on the second ship was entirely different. There we toiled long hours and took great pride in our work. It was the same enlisted crew on both ships. The officers, not the crew,

Catch your people doing something right, and let them know you appreciate it.

Example is the school of mankind, and they will learn at no other.

Edmond Burke

46

made the difference. On the second ship they set the example by working longer hours than the enlisted men. Little time was spent drinking coffee. Instead, the officers dedicated themselves to supporting our efforts by ensuring we had proper equipment and supplies. They went out of their way to encourage us and reward good performance. We always seemed to have the best food and latest movies of all the ships in the Atlantic fleet.

What happens if after setting a positive example, you still are unable to inspire the poor performer to change for the better? This is when you should employ the disciplinary approach as outlined in chapter seven.

As you begin your task of improving your coaching performance by asking the proper questions, encouraging and reinforcing behavioral change and by setting an example of excellence, keep in mind that the payoff is great. Besides contributing to the success of your organization, you will have participated in the most satisfying part of any leader's job — the growth and development of people. This is the highest calling of leadership. There is no greater monument at the end of one's career than the performance of those individuals who have reached their potential because of your leadership.

There is no more noble occupation in the world than to assist another human being—to help someone succeed.

Alan Loy McGinnis, ***Bringing Out The Best In People.***

5

The Effective Leader Insists On Excellence

Great leaders are never satisfied with current levels of performance. They constantly strive for higher and higher levels of achievement.

On the shelf in my office I keep a framed sketch of a sloppily dressed businessman with a button on his jacket reading "Mr. Good Enough." The drawing is titled: "The Enemy of Excellence." Good enough **is** the enemy of excellence! When excellence is defined as zero defects, error-free paper work processing or 100% on-time servicing of customers, any other performance level is unacceptable.

In corporate America the prime example of the "good enough" philosophy has been the 95% quality standard. For years many manufacturing firms consciously established rejection rates at 5%. Most executives believed this was a tolerable level for customers and a way to avoid substantial additional costs. The problem is that the Japanese changed the rules by deciding to compete on price **and** quality. While most American firms rested on their laurels at a 95% quality rate, the Japanese were busy finding ways to improve it to 97%, 99% and ultimately to 100%.

This philosophy of excellence is described in Toyota's *Basic Management Handbook:*

> The only acceptable quality percentage is 100%. Every car must be manufactured **exactly** according to specifications. No Toyota should **ever** leave the factory without passing quality tests perfectly.[1]

Breaking through the "good enough" barrier to enter the zone of excellence requires total preoccupation with quality from everyone in the organization. It starts with the leader's attitude.

48

If he or she insists on excellence, it will more than likely be obtained. This is called a "self-fulfilling prophecy."

In a classroom experiment with grade school children, one teacher was told she had a group of "spurters" — those that had a strong potential for high academic achievement. The truth was that they were average. Another teacher was told she had a group of slow learners. Actually, they were also average. The result of the experiment: the "spurters" progressed much more rapidly than the "slow" group.[2]

The intelligence level of both groups was the same. What made the performance difference was how the teachers related to their students. Each teacher had a different expectation of how the children would perform and treated them accordingly. The "spurters" responded to their teacher's high expectations by paying more attention in class and studying harder at home. The children in the second group became bored with the slow, repetitious nature of the instruction.

Effective leaders bring out the best in people by stimulating them to achieve what they thought was impossible.

The people in my life for whom I have the most gratitude (such as my parents, a college professor named Libby Reed, and my first boss Bill Wade) expected a great deal from me and pushed me relentlessly toward excellence. At times I certainly did not appreciate their interest in me, but now I realize that they cared enough to challenge me.

Expect the best and you will get it!

Often, merely expecting the best is insufficient to obtain desired results. People frequently need to be **shown** that the seemingly impossible performance level **is** possible.

For years no one believed it possible to run the mile race under four minutes. Until 1954, the best time ever was 4:01.4 by Gunder Haegg in 1945. Conventional wisdom held that the heart just could not stand the added stress of running any faster. Then Roger Bannister proved it could be done with a shocking time of 3:59.4. In a short time period thereafter twenty-six different men broke the four minute barrier.[3]

Similarly in 1984, the Federal Express field organization was having difficulty improving the accuracy of airbill documents. Airbill accuracy was important because the data from it was used to prepare customer invoices, but the error rate continuously

Excellence is best described as doing the right things right — selecting the most important things to be done and then accomplishing them 100% correctly.

hovered around 10% no matter how much pressure was exerted on the managers.

Finally, out of sheer frustration I decided to try a new approach. I called one of our managing directors and asked him to do a favor for me. He said, "What's on your mind?" I replied, "The airbill error rate is really killing us. Would you please take several of your stations and ask the employees there to figure out a way to improve the accuracy to at least 99.5%. When you succeed, I'd like to use their approach as the model for the entire system."

In about forty-five days the director called and said, "I've got good news! We did it even better than you asked. There were only fifty-one errors all month out of the 21,000 airbills submitted."

When the other station managers learned of the big breakthrough in the two stations, it wasn't long before the system error rate improved from 10% to .5%.

Besides showing people that major turnarounds in performance are possible, the leader should set the example for excellence in everything that he or she does. Employees will not respond to requests for better and better results from a leader who does not expect the same from himself or herself.

Here are a few additional tips for securing excellence in your organization:

1. **Become obsessed with high-quality achievement.** This means that you constantly make quality improvement your number one priority.

   Over the years I have seen many quality improvement programs come and go. Most of them had short lives. Those that were successful in the long run had one common denominator — leaders who day-in-day-out stressed quality above everything else.

2. **Recognize and make heroes out of employees who achieve exceptional quality results.** Soon other employees will emulate the heroes' behaviors. See pages 29-31 for specific ways to reward high achievers.

3. **Attack the root causes of poor quality.** Why is it so important to attack the root causes or fundamental reasons for poor

If we take care in the beginning, the end will take care of itself.[4]

quality? The answer is it is far less costly to do the job right the first time than to fix the problem later. For example, it only takes a moment for the Federal Express carrier to check the accuracy of the airbill at the point of pickup. At this time the customer is usually available to straighten out any errors or misunderstandings. Attempting to do this at a later date involves expensive telephone and clerical time plus the possible loss of customer goodwill.

In auto manufacturing the elimination of a production defect on the assembly line may cost $2.00 a car. If the dealer has to make good on the defect, the cost could easily reach $50.00.

The lesson here is obvious—take whatever actions are necessary to do the job right the first time.

Techniques For Achieving Excellence From Effective Leadership

I   MAKE QUALITY YOUR NUMBER ONE PRIORITY.

II   DEFINE EXCELLENCE AS ZERO DEFECTS, ZERO ERRORS AND ZERO FAILURES.

III   INVOLVE EVERYONE IN PLANNING AND IMPLEMENTING QUALITY IMPROVEMENTS.

IV   SHOW SUBORDINATES HOW TO ACHIEVE EXCELLENCE.

V   INSIST ON EXCELLENCE.

VI   SET THE EXAMPLE FOR EXCELLENCE.

VII   MAKE HEROES OUT OF EMPLOYEES WHO ACHIEVE EXCEPTIONAL RESULTS.

VIII   ATTACK THE ROOT CAUSES OF POOR QUALITY.

IX   DO THE JOB RIGHT THE FIRST TIME.

6

The Effective Leader Sets The Example For Others To Follow

*Example is not the main thing in influencing others. It is the **only** thing.*

Albert Schweitzer

Several days after addressing our Western Region managers on the topic of leadership, I received a note from one of the participants thanking me for inspiring him. He closed by saying, "I've always admired your style of total integrity, rigidity of purpose, and your being a good family man and a gentleman. To these qualitites do I espouse as a future executive."

Prior to receiving the manager's letter, I had not fully realized the extent that leaders influence and shape the attitudes and behavior of their followers. Most ambitious young people desire to someday reach the top of their organizations. They will model their behavior after what they observe in their leaders. If their leaders demonstrate high levels of integrity, fairplay, hardwork and teamwork, they will consider these traits necessary and will act accordingly.

My father once told me something that I will never forget. He said, "Fred, by your deeds you'll be known." What he was saying was that what you **do** as a leader exerts far more influence on employees or colleagues than what you say.

Around your employees you are constantly on stage. Everything you do is interpreted as acceptable behavior for them to emulate. If you work hard and are conscientious, others will follow suit. If you follow the rules and adhere to corporate and division policies, your people will be encouraged to do the same.

You can never afford to let down in front of your people. If you show discouragement or express a negative attitude, others will consider it acceptable to do the same.

People are changed, not by coercion or intimidation, but by example.

In short, the example you set, both positive and negative, will establish the standards for your organization.

What are some of the ways you can set an example worth emulating by your people?

1. **Become totally committed to doing the best job possible.** Throw yourself into your work. Perform assignments with a high degree of enthusiasm. Do **more** than you are asked — even if it involves some personal inconvenience, such as occasionally working at night or on a weekend.

   Lou Holtz, head coach of the Notre Dame football team, recalls that he accepted the top position with the New York Jets several years ago without being totally committed to taking the Jets to the Super Bowl. The result was that the Jets failed miserably, and he was released after eight months.

   Pete Rose, who holds the record for the most career baseball hits, credits much of his success to his father, Henry Francis Rose. "Giving 100% was not enough for him," Pete recalls. "Dad figured if the other guy gave 100%, you wouldn't win. So he made me give 110%."[2]

   Barbara Jordon, the first black Congresswoman from Texas, once said, "Each day you have to look into the mirror and say to yourself, 'I'm going to be the best I can no matter what it takes'."

2. **Build your staff with the highest quality people** — not only in terms of their knowledge and skills, but their morals and integrity. Put them in key positions where they can be the greatest help in building a corporate culture known for its professionalism and ethics. I have always felt that the true measure of a leader is the quality of people he or she selects as subordinates and advisors.

3. **Maintain a cheerful pleasant attitude.** This is one of the finest things you can do for your employees. It sets the tone for how they should treat each other. President Eisenhower, with his boyish grin, had a knack for getting people to do what he wanted without appearing gruff or upset. I am convinced that you can be just as decisive and firm with a pleasant look on your face as you can with a scowl.

4. **Refrain from "passing the heat"** up to your superiors when you have a disagreeable job to do, such as introducing an un-

Commitment is the stuff character is made of, the power to change the face of things.[1]

popular new policy or program. A weak leader will try to avoid the criticism of his or her employees by saying, "I had no choice in the matter," or "This came down from headquarters, and they're insisting it be done." As a member of management, it is the leader's job to fully understand the reasons for new policies and procedures and to effectively sell them in an empathic but firm manner, avoiding all reference to who requested the change.

There are no mistakes so great as that of being always right.

Samuel Butler

5. **Be willing to say, "I made a mistake" or "I don't know."** If you criticize an employee and later discover that he was right, you should immediately go to that person and apologize for your error. Thomas Watson, Jr., the former chairman of IBM, on one occasion went so far as to go from his office to a person's home to apologize for an insult.[3]

Executives who are unable to own up to mistakes place their welfare above that of the company. They have the mistaken belief that somehow they will lose their status and respect if they reveal an imperfection. They seem to be compelled to be infallible.

There is something refreshing and appealing about an executive who occasionally makes himself vulnerable to criticism by saying, "I was wrong," or "I don't know." Besides, being defensive and always trying to prove you are right wastes valuable energy that could be more appropriately deployed in a positive manner.

One trait that made Abraham Lincoln a great leader was his open-mindedness and willingness to admit his mistakes. Unlike other people who react defensively, Lincoln had a high degree of self-confidence and humility that enabled him, when necessary, to change course or reverse himself. During the Civil War he signed a directive to transfer several regiments from one battle sector to another. When Edwin M. Stanton, the Secreary of War, heard about the order, he refused to obey it saying, "Lincoln is a damn fool." When Stanton's remark was passed on to Lincoln, he reacted by acknowledging, "I must be wrong because Stanton is far more knowledgeable in military matters." Later Lincoln met with Stanton and reversed the order.[4]

Most young managers interested in developing themselves

are thirsty to learn from the experiences of respected leaders. Of particular interest are the details of the errors that these role models made and what was learned from them. Instead of being secretive about the past, leaders should talk openly and honestly about it. Anecdotes of victories and failures can give hope and encouragement to subordinates faced with difficult leadership problems.

6. **Avoid indiscreet, negative criticism of subordinates, colleagues and superiors.** In other words, be loyal. No matter how disloyal you feel, never express it. You can expect that even a mildly critical statement about your boss will eventually get back to him or her.

How easy it is to sit back and criticize the performance of another person or department! Yet, it is quite another thing to make positive suggestions for improvement. Will Rogers summed it all up by saying, ''There is nothing as easy as denouncing. It don't take much to see that something is wrong, but it does take some eyesight to see what will put it right again.'' Therefore, avoid participating in conversations that focus on how bad things are in other areas of the company. Instead, put all your energy into making your department or section the best.

7. **Work hard and smart.** Most successful leaders not only work hard, but have a knack of working on the right projects. They always have an agenda of important tasks they want to accomplish each day. And the important areas are related to the overall objectives of their companies and the priorities of their bosses. For more information on how to work smart by focusing your attention and making every minute count, refer to Chapter Twelve.

One universal trait that distinguishes leaders from followers is their level of energy. Leaders seem to possess enormous amounts of it. The average person works from forty to forty-five hours a week and comes home to a leisurely dinner and several hours of television. Leaders usually spend fifty to sixty hours at the office, frequently attend company and civic functions at night, and devote numerous leisure hours reading journals and books that broaden their horizons.

Resolve that whatever you do you will bring the whole man to it; that you will fling the whole weight of your being into it.

Orison S. Marden

8. **Never get involved in the dark side of office politics,** such as maligning associates, practicing deceit, manipulating others or withholding information to enhance your position. Although you may be successful in doing these things for a while, it will not take long for your colleagues to identify your true nature and turn against you. However, it is natural and normal to be an active participant in the political process that occurs in every organization which involves trying to influence others, networking and exercising power.

   The issue, therefore, is not the degree of involvement in office politics, but how you play the game. If you strive to unselfishly assist co-workers, stay on congenial terms with them and refrain from the dark side of politics, you can exert infuence without compromising your ethics. Moreover, the example you set will encourage others to follow suit.

9. **Stand up for the principles you believe in.** People trust leaders who make known their convictions and stick by them. I am not talking about pushing beliefs on others as some religious and political groups do. Instead, I am referring to taking a stand on the issues of the day and not being afraid to hang in there when the going gets a little difficult. President Lincoln was a prime example of a leader who did this. Over the years he unwaiveringly stood by his conviction that the Union must be preserved even if it meant civil war.

   On a personal note, my strong belief in the equality of all people has led me not to join any country club or private organization that does not allow minority members. I also make it a point not to participate in racial, religious and sexist jokes. **Even the hint of prejudice of any type has no place in a well run organization.**

10. **Keep an open mind** when someone questions the way you handled something or criticizes your work. Try to view such input as information only. Do not take it personally. You are free to reject it or use it as you see fit.

    No one in a leadership position is immune from criticism. In fact, the higher you go in an organization, the more you can expect. The trick is to sort out the negative feedback that is valid which can help you improve your performance from

Keep true, never be ashamed of doing right; decide on what you think is right, and stick to it.

George Eliot

The trouble with most of us is we would rather be ruined by praise than saved by criticism.

Dr. Norman Vincent Peale

that which is malicious and counterproductive.

11. **Be diplomatic** in resolving conflicts with others. An occasional dispute with an associate is bound to arise. Resolving the matter with a minimum of friction depends on how skilled you are at negotiating. Avoid the tendency that some managers have to always achieve total victory. Sticking with an ''all or nothing'' strategy too long frequently yields nothing. Select your battles. Try to win the important ones and compromise on the insignificant ones.

Winning a single battle may cause you to lose the entire war. Both parties in a dispute or conflict must feel they got something from the negotiations. Otherwise, they will remain bitter and look for ways to get even in the future. It is a wise leader who occasionally lets others win — even when he or she has the power to prevent it.

When you disagree with a recommendation, never attack it head-on by saying it is wrong or ill-conceived. Instead, present a case for another approach that you believe will better serve the needs of the business.

12. **Maintain a positive mental attitude.** Others like to be associated with a leader who has a positive outlook about life and who has a sense of direction. To have such attitudes, you must first believe in yourself and your ability to win . . . to visualize success at all times . . . to think of yourself as a champion. Dr. Norman Vincent Peale calls this ''positive imaging.'' He once told me that the key to success is ''holding in your conscious mind what you want to achieve and then striving in everything you do to make the image reality.'' William James, the noted psychologist, said, ''The greatest discovery of my generation is that man **can** alter his life style simply by altering his attitude of mind.'' Walt Disney put it another way: ''If you can dream it, you can do it.'' People can accomplish almost anything in life if they believe strongly enough that they **can** do it. Raymond Berry, Hall of Fame end for the Baltimore Colts in the 1960's, made it a practice the night before each game to spend several hours mentally rehearsing pass patterns and visualizing successful completions. Before I give a major speech, I

What you hold in your imagination about yourself, you will become.

do similar preparation by thinking about the major points I want to make and how I will present them.

Having a positive mental attitude is of particular importance if you have suffered a serious setback at work, such as losing a coveted promotion or receiving a poor performance appraisal. You can have all the ability and drive in the world; but if you do not believe you can overcome failure, you have little chance of making a comeback.

Just as success comes to those who constantly hold positive mental images in their minds, failure comes to those who are preoccupied with negative thoughts. The latter has become known as the "Wallenda Factor." In 1978, while traversing a high wire in downtown San Juan, Puerto Rico, the famous aerialist Karl Wallenda fell to his death. Later his wife told reporters that her husband was obsessed with the feeling that he would fall. "All Karl thought about for three straight months prior to it was falling."[5] He was so concerned about his safety that he personally supervised the installation of the tightrope — something he had never done before.[6] By focusing on the negative Wallenda lost his concentration and made a fatal mistake.

How does one go about the task of overcoming negative thinking? I have found that the best approach is to train yourself to recognize each negative thought that enters your mind. Then immediately replace the negative thought with a positive one on the same subject. For example, if you find yourself dwelling on how impossible it is to achieve a revenue or cost target because you do not have the necessary resources to do so, stop and say to yourself: "That's negative thinking." Then immediately begin to consider how to accomplish the mission in other ways, such as by redirecting present resources and by establishing different priorities. Another example: The next time you catch yourself complaining about traveling so much, recognize your negative thoughts and then begin considering how valuable the trips are in broading your horizons and in learning first-hand about what needs to be done to improve the performance of your operation.

Nothing can stop the man with the right mental attitude from achieving his goal; nothing on earth can help the man with the wrong mental attitude.

W. W. Ziege

13. **Develop a professional, energetic image.** Always dress conservatively and speak correctly. John T. Molloy, author of *Dress for Success* and *Molloy's Live for Success,* interviewed hundreds of executives to determine their views about success. Nearly everyone agreed that "a person who dresses conservatively, speaks standard English and carries himself in an erect manner has a better chance of succeeding than someone who does not."[7] Such habits suggest self-confidence and authority; both are important leadership traits.

    Besides maintaining a business-like appearance, develop an energetic look. Be alert, walk purposely and sit upright. If you look and act as if you have an important mission to fulfill, your employees will take their own work seriously.

14. **Be a team player.** If the people who report to you see how well you cooperate and assist executives on your level, they will be inclined to follow suit. There is no place in an organization for the overly ambitious person who only looks out for number one.

    The best way to channel your ambition is to be ambitious — not for yourself — but for your department or organization. Put all your energies into accomplishing team goals first. After that, all the other things like your recognition and advancement will take care of themselves.

    Being a team player requires that you subordinate your own personal interests and ambitions to those of the organization to which you belong.

    Selfish superstars contribute little to the success of a business enterprise. For this reason they are seldom promoted to top management. I once asked a senior officer at Kraft Foods about his secret of success. His reply: "Being helpful to my colleagues and letting them take credit for the results."

15. **Be enthusiastic.** Every organization needs a cheerleader. People are attracted to upbeat personalities, and a leader's enthusiastic spirit brings out the same in others.

    Everyone has down days from time to time. At the Mary Kay Cosmetics Company the managers are taught to "fake it until you make it," or to act enthusiastic until they feel better.

Aim for service, not success, and success will follow.

Bits & Pieces
January, 1987

Every great and commanding moment in the annals of the world is the triumph of some enthusiasm.

Ralph Waldo Emerson

16. **Treat your employees as you would like to be treated — with respect and dignity.** In a survey, employees from various companies were asked to identify the qualities that they most wanted from their jobs. The number one response. "Co-workers who treat them with respect."[8]

    A synopsis of a research study printed in the *New York Times* indicated that there is a strong correlation between a person's self-image and whether or not he treats others with respect and dignity. It follows then that if you as a leader can raise the self-image of your personnel, they will respond favorably to fellow employees and customers.

    Far too many executives give only lip service to the concept of treating all levels of employees as they would like to be treated. The widespread use of executive dining rooms, separate wash rooms and designated parking spaces only fosters a feeling of separation or estrangement between management and hourly personnel. How many managers punch a time clock when they arrive at work each morning? Very few. And yet, hourly personnel are expected to punch-in to account for their time so they do not cheat. Treating people with respect and dignity means you cannot allow some groups in your organization to feel suspect, unappreciated and shut-out. Effective leaders demonstrate sensitivity to this issue by maintaining a low profile in their business affairs and by placing the welfare of their employees above their own.

17. **Build networks.** The informal network in a company is just as important as the formal network. Much of your success as a leader depends on the willingness of people in other parts of the company to help you by providing information and by supporting your programs. The degree of such support depends on how well you are liked and trusted.

18. **Learn to keep your mouth shut.** Loose lips sink careers! Over the years I have seen many careers ruined by careless talk. As Michael Korda, Editor-in-Chief of Simon and Schuster, says, "Learn to keep quiet and look wise—people will naturally suppose that you know more than you probably do. Don't gossip and don't talk about your plans. A reputa-

A great leader never sets himself above his followers except in carrying responsibilities.

Jules Ormont

tion for keeping secrets far outweighs the easy popularily that retailing gossip may win you. The further you go in your career, the more true this is. In higher management, secrecy is golden.''[9]

19. **Avoid the ever present danger of becoming too comfortable in your job.** This happened to Rocky Balboa in the movie *Rocky III*. With considerable wealth from product endorsements and speaking engagements, he lost the competitive edge of a hungry, up and coming fighter. It was only after near ruination that Rocky decided to regain ''the eye of the tiger.''

Exceptional leaders realize that when things are going well they should become concerned. At this point the natural human tendency to let down occurs. Remember that the competition is probably staying up nights trying to figure out ways of beating you. It is a highly competitive world, so keep learning, keep hustling and keep dreaming up new and better ways of doing things.

20. **Never! Never! Never! Never! Give up.** Believe it or not, these six words comprised an entire speech by Winston Churchill. They say it all.

In summary, your subordinates and peers know you like a book. Your likes, dislikes, feelings, beliefs and attitudes become common knowledge. How your employees perceive you as a person will determine if they like you, respect you or just tolerate you. The type of example you set goes a long way toward determining which viewpoint they will adopt.

At the same time, this does not mean that you must be perfect in everything you do. You have feelings and emotions like everyone else. Occasionally, you will lose your cool or say something you later regret.

The important thing is that you learn from your mistakes and strive to be considerate of others at all times.

As a manager you're paid to be uncomfortable. If you're comfortable, it's a sure sign you're doing things wrong.

Peter Drucker

7

The Effective Leader Holds Subordinates Accountable

Anybody who accepts mediocrity — in school, on the job, in life — is a person who compromises, and when the leader compromises, the whole organization compromises.

Charles Knight, Chairman, Emerson Electric Co.

In chapter four I discussed how a leader can coach employees into improving their performance. Yet, coaching alone will not always work. An effective leader encourages employees, but also holds them accountable.

Most people are accustomed to being held accountable for their actions and the consequences of **their** failures. Leaders, on the other hand, are held accountable for **both** their own actions and those of their subordinates. Leaders must be able to accept criticism when their people make mistakes even though they, as leaders, were not directly involved in causing the failures. Once you accept this philosophy, you are on your way to becoming an effective leader.

An effective leader is tough-minded when it comes to obtaining results from subordinates. Excuses are not tolerated when **achievable** goals are not met. What counts are the **results,** not that the person really tried. If an employee does not measure up after retraining and repeated warnings, the leader must have the fortitude to take appropriate disciplinary action.

The use of the word discipline does not satisfactorily describe what the effective leader does to hold subordinates accountable. It implies the exclusive use of punishment as the motivator. The accountability approach recommended in this chapter combines certain facets of coaching with traditional disciplinary methods.

When deficiencies are first spotted, you must find out who is responsible and hold them accountable. If you ignore substandard work, it becomes the acceptable or normal way of operating.

A development-oriented leader pushes people beyond the threshold of their self-imposed limits toward their own unrealized potential.

Lyman Wood, President, Brennan College Services, Inc.

Permissiveness is neglect of duty.

Zig Ziglar

An effective leader is able to deal with occasionally being unpopular or even disliked by some people.

Before you call an employee in to discuss a performance concern that has not been corrected by coaching, be sure to get all the facts about the problem. Inexperienced managers often jump to conclusions based on incomplete information. There are always two sides to a story. So never accuse or blame a person until you have heard his side.

If after securing the facts and listening to the employee you are still displeased, you need to let him know how you feel. If you are angry, upset or frustrated, let it be known. Look the employee straight in the eye and say, "I have given you about as much latitude as possible, and now it is up to you to get your act together." Just telling the offender to fix the problem is insufficient. The person may need further advice on how to do so. There should be a clear understanding of what will happen next if the desired results are not obtained.

During such accountability sessions I find it useful to let the person know that I really want him to succeed and that I will go out of my way to provide the necessary support and assistance to do so. Also, I always make it a point to close the meeting with some words of hope and encouragement, such as, "I know you're capable of doing better," or "I am confident you can correct the problem." For the individual to make the effort to change and improve, he must believe that all is not lost and that you will keep an open mind about the future.

Sometimes the counseling approach does not work and stronger action is necessary. It may be appropriate to write a letter of concern or warning. Such letters should detail performance deficiencies and outline the expected results during the next three to six months. With such letters it is a good idea to include the ways that you intend to help the employee improve. Once again, it is important that the offender realize that there is still hope that he can regain good standing. The best way to get that message across is to say that you will remove the letter of concern from his file in six months **if** there is substantial performance improvement. Make it clear in the letter that "continued substandard results will cause further disciplinary action up to and including termination." **Never send or give such a letter to someone without first discussing it in person.**

After giving a written reprimand you can expect the offender

64

to be upset and unhappy with you. He may launch a campaign to discredit you with other employees or even your superiors. At this point you need to have the courage to take some heat. Stand firm. Others will soon realize that you acted fairly and had the best interests of the group at heart.

If the warning letter does not stimulate improvement, the next step should be to give the individual time off without pay. Normally, a day or two is sufficient to demonstrate the seriousness of the problem. It has been my experience that this strong demonstration of resolve to reject substandard performance works in some cases and not in others. Some employees will return from their days off with an entirely new attitude and a strong determination to improve. Others will harbor deep-seated animosity and will look for ways to get even.

If time off does not work, termination is usually necessary. Still, possibly one final action can be taken to stimulate the individual to change. Sometimes an unorthodox approach will get results when everything else fails. One idea is to give the offender a day off **with pay** for him to think about the seriousness of the performance problem and to develop a written correction plan. Some people respond favorably to this last chance gesture by returning to work with renewed dedication. If the plan is not followed, the individual has no one to blame but himself.

On other occasions, you may have to try a more direct approach. When I was a manager for Sealtest Foods, I employed a route deliveryman named Joe who had the habit of abusing overtime. When it was apparent that his work week would run over forty hours, he did everything possible to stretch out the remaining hours and thus maximize his overtime. I "coached" him, but he ignored my efforts. Finally, I told Joe that I would ride with him for several days to do a comprehensive time and motion study. After the second day it was obvious to both of us that the route could easily be covered within a normal forty hour week. I then prepared a report of my findings and requested a meeting with Joe and my boss. When Joe realized that I intended to pursue the matter, he admitted he was wrong and indicated that he would shape-up in the future.

Before terminating an employee you might also consider reassigning him. Perhaps another job will be more suited to his

In every organization there are some people (sometimes as high as 20%) who will not respond to anything you do. They just don't care!

65

abilities. Too often, talented employees are misplaced in jobs that are unchallenging or too demanding. They may prefer a job more suited to their talents, even if it is a demotion.

After exhausting all corrective means without results the only alternative left is to let the employee go. Since this is a drastic step, accomplish it with sensitivity and care. A former boss once gave me this advice: "I know it's difficult to terminate someone, but there eventually comes a point when the welfare of the entire group suffers if the rotten apple is allowed to remain in the barrel." Remembering this comment has helped me sleep nights when confronted with the difficult job of disciplining nonperformers.

I need to make one final point about holding people accountable by administering an escalating form of discipline: a serious problem exists with the leader if he has to frequently discipline employees. If this occurs, the leader has probably failed to earn the respect and loyalty of his people. An effective leader seldom has to use his power, but the employees know he will do so if necessary.

8

The Effective Leader Has Courage

Outstanding leaders "plug-in" to power sources external to themselves.

Courage is the intangible leadership quality of which greatness is made. It is demonstrated when a person endures severe pressure, conflict or adversity with grace and dignity. All exceptional leaders seem to have their fair share of it.

How does someone acquire courage? There is no simple formula for doing so. Nevertheless, I have come to the conclusion that an individual's continued courage under trying circumstances comes from spiritual strength. As Cicero said, "A man of courage is also full of faith." Those who believe in God or something more powerful than themselves are better able to face adversity straight on and inspire others by doing so.

Let us look at some of the ways leaders demonstrate their inner strengths. First, they do not suffer from the crippling need to be loved by everyone. For example, they are not afraid to say "no" to unreasonable requests and demands placed on them and to take positions on issues of importance. When such issues arise, courageous leaders do not remain on the sidelines by keeping quiet. Instead, they strongly express their opinions. Though they may be disliked and ridiculed from time to time, they continue to stand up for their beliefs.

Our greatest glory is not in never failing, but in rising every time we fail.

Confucius

Second, leaders have the courage to pick themselves up after defeat and work even harder than before. Successfully leading an organization every day is a tough game. You do not always meet your objectives. Occasionally you will get in hot water with your boss or associates. Even those with a high batting average are going to strike our periodically.

67

General George Washington, for example, made a series of initial mistakes in conducting the Revolutionary War against the British. At one point it was thought that the war would be lost. Yet, Washington learned from his errors, adopted new strategies and eventually prevailed. When Lee Iacocca was fired by Henry Ford in 1978, Iacocca could have retired to a life of luxury. Instead, he decided to keep going by taking the ailing Chrysler Corporation from near bankruptcy to prosperity.

I have never known a successful business leader who did not have at least one incident of serious failure in his or her career. Good leaders have the courage to take risks, to face failure and to learn from each mistake. When failure is viewed from this perspective, it becomes a stepping stone to the future.

Future triumphs are often born from past mistakes.

People generally do not learn much from their successes; they learn more from their mistakes. They gain new insights and perspectives about themselves by reflecting on what they did wrong and how they can improve in the future.

Third, leaders have the courage to face inevitable conflict openly and head on. Whenever strong-willed people interact on a frequent basis, there will be occasional disagreements and conflict. The effective leader recognizes that this is a fact of life and does not shy away from conflict because of the tension and stress involved.

In 1946, Branch Rickey, President and General Manager of the Brooklyn Dodgers, decided to face inevitable conflict by doing what was right — integrating major league sports. The signing of Jackie Robinson to a Dodger contract sent shock waves through the baseball world. At first, some of the Dodgers refused to play with Robinson. There was a threat of strikes by the Cardinals, Cubs and Phillies. Hate mail was abundant, and some of Rickey's colleagues would not speak to him. Amidst all this ridicule and conflict, Branch Rickey never waivered from his deep-rooted belief in equal opportunity for all people and in his personal support for Jackie Robinson.[1]

Occasionally, some conflict is necessary in an organization to get things moving — to obtain action where there are bureaucratic road blocks or procrastination. In explaining this principle to my staff I use an analogy: "A little friction is often needed to get traction." The trick is to keep the conflict controlled so as not to create warring factions that undermine cooperation.

Fourth, leaders have the courage and strength to bear their burdens. The best example of courage that I have ever witnessed was that demonstrated by Don Harrison, my father-in-law, as he fought his battle with terminal cancer. Never once during his long illness did he complain to his loved ones. He was always positive and thinking of others to the very end. He was an inspiration to everyone who knew him.

Finally, leaders have the courage to adapt and change as conditions and situations merit. This is not an easy task for leaders who have been successful over the years by doing things their own way. The reasoning of such people goes something like this: "Why change? I've been successful in the past."

Still as everyone knows, success is fleeting in our rapidly changing business environment. What was appropriate a few years ago may not work today. Just look what happened to the Great Atlantic and Pacific Tea Company and the International Harvester Company. Fifty years ago Wall Street considered both firms the darlings of American business. Unable to change with the times, Harvester is no longer in the farm equipment business and A & P has closed many of their stores.

There is another reason why people fail to adapt and change: most of us prefer the established routine. We are all creatures of comfort. We like the familiar because we can count on it. Surprises are uncomfortable, and change creates uncertainty. This leads to tension and stress.

One area where American business leaders have been slow to change is in reducing unnecessary overhead. Lulled into a sense of security by continued prosperity, many executives keep adding layers of management and staff support personnel. It is not until competitors demonstrate that they can produce high quality products with much lower overhead that these executives react by finding ways to do with less.

The propensity to add management and staff personnel occurs, I believe, because the reward systems in most companies encourage empire building. Normally, executive pay grades and the size of annual bonuses are determined by formulas that favor executives with the largest budgets and the most subordinates. It is

The measure of a man is the way he bears up under misfortune.

  Plutarch

When you're through changing, you're through.

  Bruce Barton

rare that a leader has the courage to cut salary costs when those cuts, though good for the company, may mean a smaller bonus or a lower pay grade.

In this chapter leadership courage was identified as a person's perseverance and determination when faced with adversity or an unusual challenge. Such courage is demonstrated in many ways, such as:

- being able to say "no" and take positions on important issues,
- responding to defeat by trying even harder,
- facing conflict openly and head on,
- bearing one's burdens and
- adapting to change.

Courage is an opportunity that sooner or later is presented to all of us.

John F. Kennedy
Profiles In Courage

9

The Effective Leader Shows Confidence In People

Few things help an in-dividual more than to place responsibility upon him, and to let him know you trust him.

Booker T. Washington, **Up from Slavery**

Trust is the emotional glue that binds follow-ers and leaders together.

W. Bennis & B. Nanus, **Leaders**

One of the biggest mistakes leaders make is to undersell their people by not having faith in them. Several years ago I learned a valuable lesson about leadership while working for Frank Borman at Eastern Airlines. Borman had asked me to design some slides that he needed for a corporate management confer-ence in San Juan. A week later we reviewed the finished slides with the Graphics/Photography Department employees who were to operate the projectors at the conference. After seeing the slides I suggested that an extra set be prepared for me to carry to the conference, just in case the originals were lost. Borman's response was quick and strong: "We don't need an extra set. I have full confidence that these people will not lose the slides and will do an excellent job with the presentation." You can imagine how I felt. It bothered me a great deal until I realized I had learned an important leadership principle.

You must trust your people even if it involves some risk. Ob-viously there will be situations in which you will have to withhold trust by checking on others, but for most business matters, it is wise to have faith that your subordinates will do their jobs in a competent manner. **Having trust in people builds their con-fidence and stimulates them to do their best.**

71

10

The Effective Leader Is Decisive

Successful leaders have the courage to take action where others hesitate.

Decision-making is a basic ingredient of leadership. It is not important whether the leader actually comes up with the proposed actions or simply endorses them. The key is that the leader does make decisions. He or she overcomes the fear of failing or being second-guessed. A leader gathers as many facts as possible, consults with subordinates and staff personnel and then decides on a course of action. Once the decision is made the effective leader does not waste time on second thoughts. The thrust of such a person is always forward — looking for the next challenge, focusing on the next decision.

Every effective leader occasionally makes a poor decision. When this occurs, what counts is how the leader handles the situation. Those that willingly admit their mistakes and take corrective action will usually be forgiven by the group. Most subordinates do not expect their leaders to be perfect. They are willing to accept some errors as long as the leader holds to the principle of trying to do what is right for the organization as a whole. What they do resent, however, is a leader who reverses a decision when pressured by a few vocal individuals or a special interest group.

Your decisions will always be better if you do what is right for the organization, not what is right for yourself.

In today's work environment it is imperative that subordinates be **involved**, one way or another, in the decision-making process. People in the work force are better educated and more self-directed than their elders. They do not expect to make all of the decisions themselves, but as a minimum they want to be consulted and be able to fully express their thoughts and ideas **before** important actions are taken.

Why is it so important to involve subordinates in decision making? The obvious reason, of course, is that better decisions are possible when different opinions and ideas are considered. More importantly, **people carry out decisions that they have participated in making much more enthusiastically than they carry out orders from the boss.** It has been proven over and over again that **involvement leads to commitment.**

Most effective leaders entrust able members of their department with the responsibility of solving their own problems whenever possible. Such leaders facilitate and guide this process to ensure that decisions are timely and do not adversely affect other work groups. In effect, they function as an advisor or consultant.

For most matters I use this approach by asking subordinates to study a problem and then take appropriate action. The results have been excellent, not only in the quality of decisions, but also in developing subordinates into leaders. However, I do not permit such latitude when the issue is controversial or when an unpopular decision must be made. Under such circumstances I always seek the opinions and advice of my staff and then make the decision myself. I try to give everyone a chance to be heard, to agree or disagree as they see fit. At times I deliberately encourage debate by taking an opposing position to the majority viewpoint or by asking another staff member to do so. I have found that open, spirited discussion creates a sense of satisfaction and commitment to the decisions that are eventually made. After hearing all sides and asking numerous questions I either make the decision on the spot or set a final date for doing so. This way everyone knows that action will be taken.

Obviously, you cannot please everyone with your decisions nor should you try. The important thing, once again, is that your subordinates have a say about major issues that impact them. After that I believe the leader must make the tough calls by saying, "This is what we'll do."

11

The Effective Leader Has A Strong Sense Of Urgency

The right man is the one who seizes the moment.

Goethe

A trait I look for in everyone I hire is a strong sense of urgency, for without it progress is slow. The attitude has to be, "Let's do it, and let's do it **now**!"

Back in the early 1960's when I was a management trainee for Sealtest Foods, I learned a valuable lesson about the need to take corrective action quickly. The plant where I worked had a street entrance where large milk tankers came in to off-load. Prior to entering the plant the trucks had to back across a wide pedestrian sidewalk. In my opinion this was an accident waiting to happen. Surely, it would not be long until an unsuspecting person was caught under those rear wheels. On numerous occasions I brought this to the attention of the plant manager. Nothing was done until **after** there was a serious accident. At the time I can remember saying to myself, "When I'm in charge, I'll never let this kind of thing happen, never!"

Contrast this lack of urgency with what happened years later when I was visiting the Federal Express station in Akron, Ohio. While in the office I noticed a computer message indicating that the Cleveland station, some 70 miles away, had received by mistake several perishable packages for a customer in Akron. Because it was Friday, I was concerned that the perishables would spoil if rerouted back through the Hub in Memphis for Monday delivery. I called the Cleveland Station Manager to ask him what he intended to do. His response: "I'm already working on a way to get them to the customer today." This is the attitude of a winner!

74

One of the most difficult challenges of leadership is to maintain a high degree of urgency to accomplish difficult goals year after year. I have always believed it is easier to build a winning team from scratch than to keep it continuously on top. With repeated success people tend to get complacent.

One way for a leader to avoid this problem is to periodically freshen the organization by changing subordinates' roles and responsibilities. Sometimes total reorganization is necessary. On other occasions having people rotate jobs is appropriate. The trick is to maintain a balance between organization stability and the feeling of excitement and commitment that comes from periodically taking on new challenges.

A major reorganization should not occur more frequently than every three or four years. More frequent changes create high levels of insecurity. Organizational fine tuning and minor adjustments, however, should occur as needed.

Even though you're on the right track — you'll get run over if you just sit there.

Will Rogers

Another way to overcome complacency in a work group and to rekindle a sense of urgency is to take some unusual or unexpected action. In the late 1940's, the Eastern Airlines baggage mishandling rate had deteriorated to an unsatisfactory level. Passengers were complaining bitterly. Captain Eddie Rickenbacker, Eastern's Chairman, was furious. When his usual exhortations to his officers failed to have an impact, he decided to take the situation into his own hands by calling a special meeting of management personnel in Miami. It was summer in Miami, and the weather was hot and humid. In those days air conditioning was not available. As the out-of-town managers checked into the hotel, they were told that their bags would be placed in their rooms. Instead, Rickenbacker had the bags locked up in a storage area overnight.

In his autobiography Rickenbacker tells what happened next:

> There they were for the meeting the next morning unshaven, teeth unbrushed, wearing dirty shirts. There was no sign of the baggage all day. That night it was delivered, with a great pounding on all the doors, at 3:00 a.m. At the opening session the second morning, I said, "Now you know how the customer feels when you mishandle his luggage."[1]

75

When I was the Newark Airport Station Manager for Eastern Airlines in 1977, I did something similar but less dramatic to overcome management complacency. At the time we were experiencing a rash of accidents due to operator carelessness. Too much equipment was being damaged on the ramp. It was apparent that the supervisors were not holding the operators accountable. The problem continued even after the supervisors were directed to take action.

One Sunday evening I received a call from the Control Center Manager, Dominick Zappia, informing me of another serious damage to an expensive device used to load containers into the bellies of L-1011 aircraft. This was the last straw! I told Dominick to call all the supervisors, even those at home, to tell them to report to a special meeting at 10:00 p.m. that night, even though it was Sunday, to resolve the problem once and for all. We talked into the early morning until everyone was satisfied that we had an action plan that would work.

Good leaders seldom need to take such dramatic action to get results. Their subordinates will normally correct problems when asked to do so. It is only when everything else fails that the leader should look for an unorthodox way to inspire action.

Finally, organizational complacency is avoidable if leaders maintain their own sense of urgency. It is imperative that they never let down because as soon as they do, others will quickly follow suit. Richard Sloma in *No-Nonsense Management* says, ''If the captain relaxes too long, the crew will go on vacation.''

There are a number of things leaders can do to keep up their **own** motivation and enthusiasm. The best approach is to vary your leadership focus and style periodically. Too many major changes can be confusing and threatening to subordinates, but leaders should add variety to keep the work stimulating and interesting.

Develop a new program or campaign to correct a longstanding performance deficiency. Establish goals for your department that are more challenging than those requested by your boss. Periodically change the location and agenda format of your monthly staff meetings. Start coming to work earlier than usual and leaving a little earlier. Give assignments to subordinates that you normally handle.

Occasionally, it's necessary for the leader to be unpredictable and inconsistent. If you're too predictable some people will take advantage of you.

No one keeps up his enthusiasm automatically. Enthusiasm must be nourished with new actions, new aspirations, new efforts, new vision. It is one's own fault if his enthusiasm is gone; he has failed to feed it.

Papyrus

Another approach to perk up your enthusiasm is to become an expert in a function you know little about but think you might enjoy. Pick an area of interest related to your present job. For example, if you are a sales manager, become knowledgeable about marketing or sales training. Likewise, if your firm is expanding overseas, learn about foreign cultures. In time you will be recognized for your new expertise. Others will seek your advice, which could lead to a promotion or even an entirely new career.

The idea is to try new approaches to avoid getting into the comfortable rut of doing the same thing over and over again. You will feel better about your job and others will note your positive attitude.

Of all the things a leader should fear **complacency** heads the list. To remind me of what can happen to an organization that has lost its will to win, I keep a snapshot of one of our competitor's trucks with the driver sound asleep. He should have been doing paperwork or canvassing a building for new customers.

People who keep hustling are in great demand in organizations.

The role of the leader is to keep everyone energized and inspired by (1) periodically changing or rotating subordinate responsibilities, (2) taking unusual or unexpected action and (3) setting the example of urgency for others to follow.

12

The Effective Leader Makes Every Minute Count

Time is your most valuable personal resource. Use it wisely because it can't be replaced.

Take a moment to answer the following questions:
- Do you take work home on a regular basis to keep up?
- Do you keep deferring important projects because of insufficient time to concentrate on them?
- Does excessive paperwork pile up when you are away on trips?

A "yes" answer to these questions means that you are not running the job, the job is running you. Buried in detail and lacking focus, you are neglecting the critical leadership dimension of visualizing the future and preparing for it. Instead, you constantly seem to be in a reactive or "firefighting" mode. The paperwork continues to stack up, putting you further and further behind. It is a never ending and self-defeating cycle caused by the poor management of time.

Thankfully there is a way out of this predicament. Time management skills can be developed and perfected leading to substantial improvement in your productivity.

This chapter is devoted to the presentation of techniques used by successful leaders to make the best use of their most precious commodity — time.

1. **Identify the areas of your job with the greatest payoff for your organization.** In most jobs there are a limited number of functions or activities that are critical to overall success. If these functions progress well, overall success is virtually assured. Some people call this the 80/20 rule — eighty percent of the performance results come from focusing on twenty per-

Choosing and performing activities with high leverage is the key to managerial effectiveness.[1]

Andrew S. Grove, President, Intel Corporation

Disciplined focus is what distinguishes those who make things happen from those that watch things happen.

cent of the job. For a service manager the twenty percent involves selecting quality service representatives and training them extensively. For a production manager it is ensuring that a strong quality ethic exists among all employees. Job functions that have the greatest payoff are called **critical success areas.**

2. **Develop goals for each critical success area.** These goals can be for yourself or your organization. To be meaningful, they must be: (a) challenging, (b) understandable and (c) obtainable.

The task of making goals challenging and understandable is readily accomplished by most managers. Most difficulties arise from the tendency to force subordinates to stretch too much in performance. With increasing foreign competition and the desire to keep stock prices high (to avoid unfriendly takeovers), the operating manager is under extreme pressure to maximize short-term earnings by accepting ambitious, often unrealistic productivity and cost objectives. This places him in an untenable position. It can be a no win situation. If the manager resists the goals too vigorously, he risks being branded as timid or ineffectual. At the same time, if he accepts unrealistic goals and fails, he may lose his job. Placed in such a pressure cooker, it is no wonder that some managers seek relief by compromising their standards of honesty and integrity.

The only way out of this predicament is for top management to ensure that goals are challenging, understandable **and** obtainable. This must be done even at the expense of short-term earnings.

3. **Set weekly priorities to facilitate the accomplishment of goals.** Each Friday evening before I leave work for the weekend I spend an hour or so thinking about what I want to accomplish the following week. The tasks that relate to my goals I give top ranking. These are the ''must complete'' items. Everything else is labeled ''do when possible.'' Other executives do their weekly planning Sunday evening or when they first arrive at the office Monday morning. The idea is to utilize the approach with which you are most comfortable.

The best way to insure focus on your weekly priorities is to

Nothing is as necessary for success as the single minded pursuit of an objective.

Frederick W. Smith, Chairman, Federal Express Corp.

The art of becoming wise is the art of knowing what to look over.

Wm. James

support them with daily plans. Before arriving at the office each morning take a few minutes to visualize what you want to accomplish during the day. Make a list and check off each item as it is accomplished. Doing so will give you a strong sense of accomplishment.

4. **Do the most important things first and never waste time on unimportant activities.** This sounds simple, but it is not. People tend to gravitate toward tasks that are enjoyable and avoid the difficult or disagreeable ones. Unfortunately, successful performance always entails doing some tasks you might not enjoy. The best approach is to force yourself to do these tasks first. Stick with them until they are accomplished, and then reward yourself by tackling something more pleasurable.

The best way to separate the wheat from the chaff is to constantly ask yourself, ''Does it really matter if I **do** this task or not?'' And if it does matter, ''Does it have to be done now or can it be postponed?''

5. **Concentrate on a few things at a time.** Leaders need to realize that they can only bring their special abilities to bear on a few critical success areas at one time. Therefore, focus on one or two areas that will benefit most from your leadership expertise. Stick with them until you are satisfied with the results. Then you are ready to move on to another challenge.

The amount of time you spend on a problem or a project is not what counts; rather, it is the amount of uninterrupted time. To illustrate the value of this concept, let us apply it to the problem of developing a new program to improve customer service. The way to accomplish this task efficiently is to concentrate on it without frequent interruptions.

If you cannot obtain privacy in your own office during normal hours, seek a location where you can. I find it helpful to occasionally use a vacant office or a conference room, or any location where I can concentrate without interruptions.

I also try not to schedule or attend meetings before 11:00 a.m. Prior to this time my secretary limits phone calls to those of my direct subordinates and fellow officers. All other calls are answered before I go to lunch. I call the 8:00-11:00 a.m. time period "my private time." It is routinely utilized to go over the mail, write memoranda and plan for the future. This is the only part of the day that I try to control rigidly. The remainder of the day is kept open so that I am available for meetings and appointments. My subordinates and associates have grown accustomed to this routine and respect my need for it. It does not upset them to miss me in the morning as long as they can count on meeting in the afternoon.

The "morning private time" approach has a number of benefits. First, it enables me to accomplish a great deal in a minimal amount of time. Projects that used to take days are accomplished in a few hours. Second, by reviewing the mail first, I am on top of what is going on and what is on other people's minds. This prepares me to deal with important issues during the remainder of the day. Finally, and possibly most important, the morning private time helps my morale. An ever growing stack of paperwork signifying loose ends and missed deadlines makes me frustrated and irritable.

6. **Establish deadlines for yourself.** Most people work better under a little pressure. A self-imposed deadline can provide the incentive you need to keep going at full speed. I use this technique when preparing a speech. My goal is to write a rough draft two weeks in advance of the speech. This provides ample time to improve the content and mentally rehearse the delivery.

7. **Don't be a slave to your mail.** Unattended or partially attended mail can be very distracting and can even create stress. The best way to keep this from happening is to discipline yourself to handle mail promptly and decisively. Establish a routine for processing it early in the day. Review the high priority letters and reports first, and then **take action on each item.** Toss it, return it to your secretary for filing or send it to someone else for his or her action or information. Never read a report or letter and then hold it for later handling. Such procrastination results in piles of documents requiring action.

8. **Set aside a few minutes each day to think about creative ways to improve the performance of your organization.** This may be the most valuable time you ever spend! It only

Performance break-throughs come from pondering the unthink-able.

takes an occasional creative idea to ensure the future of your department and your career.

People are most creative when they are rested and feel good. This is why you hear about the brainstorms that occur while jogging, showering in the morning or driving to work. These are excellent times to let your mind ponder what could be achieved if there were no operational or financial constraints. Think of the ideal or ultimate way to accomplish your goals. Later on you can always make this vision more practical.

Earlier in the book an effective leader was described as someone who has a vision of what is necessary for the success of an organization and who has the ability to inspire and energize others to reach that vision. In the former area many executives fall short. They do not spend enough time reflecting on what is ahead for their business units.

Ultimate leadership success, such as profitably running a company, requires both vision and the ability to inspire people; both can be developed if the individual is willing to do so.

9. **Do not arrange for or attend unnecessary meetings.** It is estimated that more than one-half of the meetings conducted in American business are unnecessary. Be very selective in the meetings that you attend. Try to limit your participation to meetings that relate to your goals. For unimportant meetings send one of your staff to represent you. Always ask that individual to send you a written summary of the meeting or brief you on the results.

If you chair meetings, keep them as brief as possible. Prepare and distribute agendas in advance. Stick to them. To encourage brevity, try scheduling meetings before lunch or late in the day. Another approach is to sandwich meetings between two scheduled appointments. Prior to starting the meeting be sure to inform everyone of the time constraint and then keep to the schedule.

For years, each Monday morning at 9:00 a.m. I conducted a review of Federal's service performance for the prior week. Representatives from all operating groups attended. We had a set rule that the meeting would last no longer than one hour. When we first invoked the rule, we had to abruptly cut off several presentations to end on time. Before long everyone realized that they had to be brief and to the point. We never exceeded the one hour limit by more than five minutes.

10. **Do not let visitors steal your valuable time.** While working in your office you cannot afford to be constantly interrupted by visitors and associates that "only want a minute of your time." Your objective should always be to keep the channels of communication open without allowing others to waste your time.

This requires that you make judgements concerning when to freely share your time with others and when to conserve time. Here are a few suggestions for conserving time by minimizing unwelcome interruptions without being impolite:

a) Remain standing when visitors or colleagues pop into your office to engage in small talk. Unless you have time, do not invite them to sit and become comfortable. People get down to business quicker when they are on their feet.

b) Be honest with people when you cannot spend time with them. Indicate you are very busy but would be glad to see them at another time.

c) Do not be timid about saying "no" to salesmen or vendors who arrive at your office without an appointment.

11. **Delegate.** Continually seek ways to give your subordinates more and more responsibility. Do not be afraid to overload them. Most people have the capacity to handle additional work, especially if it provides opportunities to prove that they are capable of more demanding jobs.

Get into the habit of asking yourself if what you're doing can be handled by someone else.

Besides helping others to develop, delegation is the key to the leader's sanity. You cannot do it all yourself. The more you try, the greater the pressure and tension. Extensive delegation also frees valuable time for you to concentrate on your goals.

There is more to delegating than meets the eye. It is insufficient to merely make assignments and wait for results. Adherence to the following rules of effective delegation will improve your performance in this important leadership function.

a) **Establish a climate that facilitates delegation.** There are two critical requirements necessary to do so. The first is mutual **trust.** You must trust that your subordinates will take their assignments seriously and do the best job possible. On the other hand, your subordinates must trust that you will give them the credit for the good results they achieve. If you have the habit of stealing the credit for yourself, do not expect excellence from your personnel.

The second requirement is **support.** People cannot be effective in their work unless they have all the pertinent data and background information. You can be most helpful in this area. Distribute copies of appropriate memoranda and reports. Spend the necessary time with your personnel discussing the background and ramifications of assignments. Take them to upperlevel meetings where they can gain perspective of broad corporate strategy. Your efforts to share all available information and make your people feel like insiders will create commitment to the assigned projects.

The idea is to stay involved in the delegation process. Do everything possible to facilitate the efforts of your personnel from the time you first assign to them a task to when they complete it. This includes giving subordinates authority to carry out assignments and ensuring that they feel free to approach you with questions.

b) **Delegate with deadlines.** When passing out assignments remember Parkinson's Law: "Work expands to fill the time available for its completion." In other words, people tend to stretch out jobs as long as they can. To avoid procrastination and delay, directives to your subordinates should **never** be open-ended. Reasonable completion dates should always be specified.

When I was with Eastern Airlines, I knew an executive who never established deadlines with subordinates. He always wondered why tasks were never completed on time.

Besides helping the leader, delegating with deadlines benefits those given assignments. It frees the leader from constantly nagging staff members to complete assignments. They then can concentrate on tasks without interference or undue pressure.

Be sure to keep deadlines realistic. If your personnel keep missing them for reasons beyond their control, they will soon start ignoring them completely.

Allow your people to put their personal stamp on projects delegated to them.

c) **Create involvement in the assignment by asking for the employee's ideas and recommendations.** People perform better when their input is valued. The **worst** thing a leader can do is to delegate with a lot of advice on how to do the job. This kills initiative and creativity. For example, if you ask a subordinate to prepare an analysis of the competitors in your industry and then proceed to tell him exactly what you want in the report, that is what you will get. Any additional information or intelligence that might have been obtained will be missing.

12. **Make every minute count for your personnel.** So far this chapter has focused on how you, the leader, can make the best use of your time. What about the time of your staff members? Theirs is valuable, too. Show consideration for them by being prompt to attend meetings. Avoid making them wait.

The best way to minimize such unproductive time is to provide some slack between your meetings and appointments just in case they run over. Your concern for the time of others will be appreciated and make them feel important too.

13. **Shield yourself from energy losses due to worrying.** Focusing on what someone else thinks of you, reorganization rumors or some imagined slight from a colleague drains valuable energy needed to lead others. The key to combating worry is to become aware of your emotions. Only then can you keep things in proper perspective.

14. **Coordinate your schedule with your secretary.** Your secretary is the key person in your business life who can help you be better organized. Spend some time with him or her each morning reviewing schedules and priorities for the day. This time investment will pay great dividends.

Do not waste your high-energy hours. Invest them where they yield the highest payoff.

15. **Learn to utilize small chunks of time** that are normally wasted, such as waiting to board an airplane, standing in line at a supermarket and waiting to pick up your kids. During such times read something of value or discuss important matters with another person. The most successful leaders never waste a moment.

16. **Get off to an early start each morning.** Possibly the most important time saving advice is to begin work early each day. Arriving at the office between 7:30 and 8:00 a.m. provides an hour or more of valuable quiet time, uninterrupted by phone calls and associates wanting to talk. People who have the habit of starting work early claim by doing so their entire day goes more smoothly.

In review, you can improve your productivity and the productivity of your people by following the principles of time management in this chapter. Improvement can be accomplished without putting in more hours yourself. You might even surprise yourself by reducing some of the evening and weekend work that you previously thought was unavoidable. Most importantly, you will have more time to concentrate on the matters that really count: your goals and interactions with your personnel.

Overemphasis on time management can be as serious a problem as poor utilization of time. Becoming more efficient and productive is certainly a worthwhile pursuit, but it should never overshadow your "people" work. With this in mind let us turn our attention to the critically important topics of becoming more effective in dealing with others. In the next three chapters you will learn:

- To earn the loyalty of subordinates,
- To become more employee-centered and
- To do a better job of listening.

13

The Effective Leader Earns The Loyalty Of Employees

Effective leaders make their followers feel good about themselves and their work.

The loyalty of your employees is priceless. It cannot be bought or secured by favors. It is not won overnight nor is it everlasting. Rather, loyalty is given by the group as long as they think their leader is worthy of it.

Here are some ways to gain and hold the loyalty of your people:

1. **Develop warm, person-to-person relationships with your subordinates.** Be approachable. This does not require that you become close personal friends. I have always felt that strong relationships can be built and maintained at work and at work alone. It is not necessary to frequently socialize after hours with your subordinates to lead them successfully.

   However, you should participate in company sponsored social events such as picnics, golf tournaments, softball games and retirement parties. It is also appropriate to occasionally take your staff members and their spouses to dinner as a group. Such activities help build teamwork and improve communications. They also help the employee's spouse feel a part of the company.

   Socializing with an **individual** subordinate, however, can be counterproductive. Some employees may feel that this person is the boss's favorite. Other subordinates who do not enjoy the same treatment could become jealous. There is also the possibility that a favored subordinate will take advantage of his or her special relationship with the boss.

   Familiarity can breed contempt and erode respect for the leader. A certain psychological barrier must be maintained

The goal of the leader should be to develop mutual respect with subordinates — not friendships.

What we have done for ourselves alone dies with us. What we have done for others and the world remains and is immortal.

Albert Pine

between the leader and the follower to ensure objectivity.

Whether or not you adopt this philosophy toward socializing privately with individual subordinates, it is vitally important that you take a sincere and genuine interest in each person while you are with them at work. Be interested in their families, hobbies, likes and dislikes and aspirations in life.

A study reported in *Advances in Experimental Social Psychology* revealed that showing genuine interest in people is the most important thing a leader can do to build and maintain the loyalty of his or her followers. The best way to show interest in people is to give them your time. Freely sharing this most precious commodity demonstrates that you really care. If you care about your people, they will care about you.

2. **Be aggressive in serving your personnel.** All leaders should remember that their **primary** mission is to help subordinates be successful in **their** jobs. Providing such service involves clearing away obstacles that hinder performance such as insufficient manpower or equipment and showing people how to do their jobs more effectively.

In addition to helping your employees succeed look for other ways to serve them. This point is best illustrated by an experience I had several years ago in Minneapolis. On a bitter cold January evening I arrived at the Federal Express station. During the short distance from the parking lot to the office I was chilled to the bone. It was difficult to breathe without the cold air causing discomfort to my lungs. Upon opening the door to the customer counter area, I found the station manager putting on a heavy parka. "Where are you going on such a horrible night?" I asked. "Please excuse me for awhile," she replied. "Some of the couriers' cars won't start, and I need to help them." I thought to myself, "What commitment to others!"

Finally, pay attention to the physical comfort needs of your personnel. A hot office, dirty restrooms or inadequate lighting might not be a big deal to you, but they can be to others. It was a wise person indeed who once said, "It's not the mountain ahead that bothers the climber, but the grain of sand in the shoe."

The leader who is sensitive to the needs of his employees is aggressive in quickly resolving minor complaints or concerns before they become major ones. If necessary, he will stick his neck out with superiors or colleagues to obtain adequate resources and assistance for his people. The old adage that the squeaky wheel gets the grease applies to this facet of leadership. Employees do not have to work in plush surroundings to be content, but they do require leaders that look after their needs.

3. **Confide in the people you trust.** It is hard to be loyal to someone who is overly secretive. An individual feels important and special whenever the boss shares information about company business that is not public knowledge.

4. **Provide special rewards for your outstanding performers,** such as large merit increases, strong recommendations for promotion and recognition from you and your boss. High achievers need such treatment or they will lose interest and look elsewhere for employment.

An excellent way to show appreciation for good work is to write letters of commendation to those who deserve credit. The advantage of letters is that the recipient can show them to co-workers, friends and family. Be sure to send a copy to your boss and any other officials who might be interested. I call this "broadcast recognition." It places your people where they belong — in the spotlight.

Unselfishly giving well-deserved credit to your people is one of the finest things you can do for them. It not only makes them feel good, but stimulates them to try even harder.

5. **Recognize and show appreciation for other employees, too.** Most leaders find it natural to recognize their high achievers. Yet, pressed with busy and demanding work schedules, you may easily overlook the many solid performers who quietly get the job done day-in, day-out. Because they do not require much supervision, the tendency is to take them for granted. These people also need to be recognized with periodic indications that their performance is acceptable and appreciated. A simple sincere demonstration of your interest in their work can go a long way toward keeping up their morale.

The best way to maintain morale is to meet individually

Effective leaders follow the basic dictum of a West Pointer: Make sure the troops are settled and fed before you take care of your own needs.

The deepest principle in human nature is the craving to be appreciated.

Wm. James

Be proud of the accomplishments of your people. Always give them credit for their successes.

with each of your subordinates at least once a week. If your staff is geographically dispersed, utilize the phone extensively. During this special one-on-one time give the employee ample opportunity and encouragement to express anything on his or her mind. Look for things that are done right and acknowledge your understanding and appreciation for them. Further, do not underestimate the power of a sincere **thank you.**

Several experiences in my career at Federal Express illustrate the power of recognition and appreciation. The first experience occurred in New York when I interviewed a courier who had received a letter of warning for excessive tardiness. I was intrigued by the fact that the person's attendance record had been excellent for a number of years prior to the recent problem. I asked him if he had personal problems at home that might have affected his ability to get to work on time. "No," he replied, "that's not the case." "What happened then to cause this sudden change in your behavior?" It took some time for the courier to spill out his feelings about not being appreciated on the job. Apparently, the work did not come easy to him, but he always tried to do his best. Never once did his manager offer a word of appreciation. "It's like I never existed in his eyes. So I did the only thing I could think of to get attention; I started coming in late. At first management didn't even realize what was happening. Now look what's happening. My boss has held several private discussions with me, and I get to talk with a Senior Vice-President!"

People thrive on the appreciation you show them — the smiles, the thanks and the gestures of kindness.

Shortly after the New York incident I was asked to speak at a district sales meeting. Prior to introducing me, the sales manager announced that she wanted to make several special recognition awards. She then proceeded to describe what each person had done and called him or her individually to the podium to receive a plaque. I will never forget the joyous expressions on the faces of those who received awards.

Stan, a manager for a major oil company, told me that he was so starved for recognition and appreciation from his boss that he once wrote on a copy of one of his oil exploration studies: "Excellent work Stan." He then sent it to a number of his peers and the vice-president of his division. This manager was so starved for recognition that he had to praise himself!

Although praise and recognition are powerful motivators, they should never be used in lieu of pay increases, benefit improvements and increased status symbols. Motivating employees requires both praise and tangible rewards. The effective leader does not stint on either.

People are motivated by the opportunity to accomplish challenging tasks.

The praise and reward, however, must be carefully selected. The successful leader determines which rewards or incentives are most meaningful to each person. What motivates one person does not necessarily motivate another. For example, a young ambitious person may crave an opportunity to be promoted to any location as long as he can move up the management ladder. Another staff member who is struggling to meet college tuition payments for his children might value large salary increases. Still another employee might simply want to know that his job is secure. The point is that the leader needs to tailor the reward system to each employee.

6. **Give your subordinates the benefit of the doubt** when problems arise affecting their performance. For example, if an employee fails in an area, do not give up on him until ample opportunity is given for improvement.

7. **Never say that you will do something for an employee and then change your mind.** As acknowledgement of such a double-cross quickly spreads throughout the organization, you will lose the loyalty of everyone.

In summary, the best way to gain and hold the loyalty of your personnel is to show interest in them and care for them, by your words and actions, in everything you do. And this attitude of concern must be sincere. Your subordinates will never be totally loyal unless they feel deep down that you are devoted to the good of all and are doing everything in your power to help them to succeed both as individuals and as a group.

14

The Effective Leader Is Employee-Centered

The great paradox of life: The more you give of yourself, the more you receive.

Employee-centered leaders are sensitive to the needs and feelings of their people. They are supportive of employees, helpful to them, and concerned for their well-being. Such leaders subordinate their own interests to those of others.

The principle focus in American business remains on the profit and loss numbers. Obviously, you cannot keep people gainfully employed unless the company is profitable. The problem arises when decisions revolve solely on the basis of cost without due consideration to the people issues involved. Worse yet are the decisions made at the expense of employees. Invariably, such short-sighted approaches do not stimulate the kind of teamwork and extra effort required to compete in today's quality-conscious markets. When employees feel abused or when they do not feel valued, they tend to do just enough to get by.

For a people-first philosophy to capture the heart and soul of an organization, it must be based on the fundamental belief and practice that people are cared for and treated with dignity first and foremost because it is the right thing to do.

David Sarnoff, former Chairman of RCA, identified the most important by-product of being employee-centered. He said, "We accomplish greatness through other people. Nothing great can be accomplished without the involvement of other individuals."

Employees will not automatically respond to the orders of a manager who tries to lead by virtue of his position or status.

The time is always right to do what is right.

Martin Luther King

They care primarily about how much he appreciates them and if he can be trusted.

Many employees, especially those in their 20's or 30's, do not have the same strong loyalty to their employers that their parents had. Young workers are likely to come and go based on pay rates, working conditions and, most importantly, the satisfaction they receive from the job. This satisfaction is derived from having interesting tasks, being involved and learning new skills — all of which lead to a feeling of worth.

Share your inner gifts with your personnel: your warmth, enthusiasm and sensitivity.

Morale and productivity are highest in work groups when the leader shows a high degree of **consideration** and **concern** for employees. This requires that the leader understand that each subordinate is the center of his or her own universe; each employee has unique needs, interests, likes and dislikes.

Most people appreciate a boss who takes a sincere interest in them, who responds in some appropriate manner to the great joys and sorrows that occur in their lives. The idea is not to be nosey and constantly prying into employees' personal lives, but to be responsive in a warm, human way when you get word of a serious personal problem.

Frank Borman, who headed Eastern Airlines from May 1975 until June 1986, went out of his way to demonstrate that he cared for his employees. In the late 1970's I worked for him as his Executive Assistant. One evening when I returned from a business trip, I found his car parked in my driveway. Obviously, I was concerned that something serious had happened as he had never visited my home. When I entered the back door, I found him playing with my four-year-old daughter Cindy, who was recovering from knee surgery. He had brought a teddy-bear to cheer her up.

Joita McGlynn, a former Eastern employee, relates another touching story about Borman. Her sister Missy, who was seriously ill, asked Joita if she could meet her "big boss." Joita took her to Miami to do so. When Borman learned of the situation, he gladly offered to see them. After talking to Joita and

Missy for a while Borman said, ''I'd now like to spend some time with Missy alone, so it will be her special time.''

Contrast these demonstrations of caring concern with an incident that occurred in another company several years later. While working on a construction site, a man was struck by a falling tile that caused cuts and lacerations. He was immediately rushed to the hospital and later released to spend several days at home to recover. A number of his co-workers sent cards and called him. Yet, the one person who counted most, his boss, never inquired about his welfare. Just as Cindy and Missy will never forget Frank Borman's thoughtfulness, the man struck by the tile will never forget his boss's insensitivity and lack of concern.

Build a reservoir of good will by placing the interests of your people above your own.

If you remember only one thought from this chapter it should be: handle an employee's problem swiftly and as seriously as if it were a problem with your own paycheck. Most of you, I am sure, have experienced a situation where **your** paycheck was late, lost or shorted. Remember how quickly you called the Payroll Department or asked your manager to straighten out the problem. Treat the problems of your subordinates with the same concern and urgency.

Being employee-centered also means being **fair** — treating others as you would like to be treated. The results of numerous surveys in major corporations point out that getting a fair deal is **the** most important concern to employees at all levels. Even the slightest hint of favoritism can poison the morale of an organization. Showing more warmth to staff members you like or spending more time with them can be demoralizing to others who perceive that they are not in your favor. The cardinal rule is: **play no favorites.**

In review, the effective leader has the ability to make others feel good about themselves by the degree of consideration, concern and equity shown. Attending to these feelings creates a strong bond between the leader and his or her followers.

15

The Effective Leader Listens To Subordinates

Make people feel important by listening carefully to them.

Listening attentively and empathically is one of the best ways to show respect for an employee. It demonstrates that you believe the individual has worthwhile thoughts and therefore is a valued member of the team. When people feel needed, they tend to take more interest in what they do.

Empathetic listening does more than facilitate employee motivation. It helps protect the leader from being blind-sided. Employees will not open up to leaders who are aloof or too busy to spend time listening. Without the knowledge of what subordinates really think and believe, the leader is vulnerable to the sudden surfacing of a major morale problem. By listening to employees' perceptions of problems, you can resolve them before they escalate.

An office manager of an accounting firm was uncomfortable relating to first-level employees. Instead of listening to them directly, he relied on his supervisors' interpretations of their concerns. Frustrated, the employees wrote their complaints to the President of the company. The problems that could have been resolved easily at a lower level of management, were now the topic of discussion with upper management.

By insulating himself from first-level personnel the manager did not know what was going on in his operation. Had he kept the channels of communication open at all levels and listened through the grapevine deep within the organization, he could have identified the problems early and taken corrective action.

According to James MacGregor Burns, "few executive leaders have better exemplified the strengths and weaknesses of personnel management than Franklin Roosevelt. Some said he had a discerning, intuitive grasp of the needs and motivations of his cabinet members and agency chiefs. One of his many traits — difficult for a man who loved to talk and dominate the scene — was to listen sympathetically to those who poured out their woes and frustrations."[1]

Whenever General Eisenhower was faced with a difficult problem, he would call his staff together and take great pains to listen to their ideas and recommendations. It is reported that President Kennedy failed to solicit adequate discussion about the Bay of Pigs issue before deciding to go ahead with the operation. He changed his approach, however, during the Cuban missile crisis when he actively sought divergent opinions before taking action.

These stories illustrate a vital principle about listening and communicating in general: **Leaders who make it a practice to draw out the thoughts and ideas of their subordinates and who are receptive even to bad news will be properly informed.** Having the straight-scoop and all the appropriate information is very important to the leader's ability to make good decisions.

All of us prefer good news to bad. Few subordinates will voluntarily present all the details of bad news if their bosses become upset and sore. Instead, there will be a tendency to cover-up or sugar-coat the facts. Leaders who follow the advice of welcoming the messenger of bad news (instead of shooting him) will be well ahead of the game in the communications area.

A number of approaches and techniques will improve your listening skills. Here are some that I find useful:

The most important good listening habit is to totally concentrate on what the person is saying.

1. Try to interpret the surface conversation of the speaker to determine his true feelings and thoughts. In the presence of the boss many employees will not open up and express what is on their minds. Instead they will couch their words to refrain from stepping on someone else's toes. Since frank communication is vital to the success of any organization, the leader must be able to draw out the feelings of subordinates by listening sympathetically.

2. Be an active listener:
   a) Assume an attentive attitude — stand up or sit up straight and maintain good eye contact.
   b) Take notes.
   c) Ask pertinent questions and rephrase key points that are made (e.g., "Do you mean that . . .," or, "My understanding of what you just said is . . ."). Do this in a manner that does not give the impression that you have already made up your mind about what was said or are looking for an argument.
3. Wait until you clearly understand what a person is saying before you reply.
4. Show respect for the individual who is talking by refraining from discourteous nonverbal behavior such as glancing at your watch, letting your eyes wander, shuffling papers or starting for the door. These actions signal a lack of interest to someone who is trying to relate something important.
5. Control your desire to do the talking. There is no way you can listen while speaking.
6. Draw out the individual by asking his opinions or ideas on a subject. If discussion on a performance problem is required, refrain from criticizing the qualities of the person such as his integrity or intelligence. Focus instead on what can be done to prevent the problem from happening again. Very little meaningful conversation occurs when people feel attacked or threatened. Throughout the conversation, convey the impression that it is okay to express deep feelings without being judged. The best way to do so is to maintain a supportive attitude.
7. Listen to everyone, not just to those whom you like or respect. It is easy to fall into the trap of giving attention to high producers and ignoring average performers. This practice can hurt morale and cause some workers to remain quiet even though they have something important to contribute.
8. Do not jump to conclusions after the first few sentences are spoken. This will make employees feel you are really not interested in what they have to say. Instead, hear them out. Only then will you fully understand what is on their minds.

9. Avoid the temptation to interrupt the other person to make your own comments or points. You may not agree with what the individual is saying, but you must allow him to say it. It is remarkable how many problems and concerns dissolve when people are given the opportunity to get things off their chests.

10. Minimize telephone interruptions by conducting important conversations away from your desk. I often do this at lunch or arrange for breakfast meetings during which I can give the other person my undivided attention. If this is impractical, have your calls held until you are free. There is nothing more distracting than a ringing phone when you are trying to discuss a serious matter.

11. Pay attention to the speaker's facial expressions and tone of voice. Watch his body language. These things may reveal hidden feelings or opinions not fully expressed.

12. Make it easy for your people to see you by spending ample time in the work area. When using your office keep the doors open unless engaged in private conversations.

Remember that when the employees no longer believe that their manager listens to them, they start looking around for someone who will.

16

The Effective Leader Is Determined

PRESS ON. Nothing in the world can take the place of persistence. Talent will not; nothing is more common than unsuccessful men with talent. Genius will not; rewarded genius is a proverb. Education will not; the world is full of educated derelicts.
Persistence and determination alone are omnipotent.

Calvin Coolidge

High-performing leaders exhibit exceptional determination in pursuing their objectives. They never let up until they succeed. A recent study of Nobel Prize winners in science revealed that what distinguishes the winners from their colleagues is remarkable determination.

There is no better example than Thomas Edison, who in April 1872 worked continuously day and night to find a way to permit simultaneous two-way transmission on a telephone line. Suffering from exhaustion, he was about ready to give up. On the twenty-second day, he found the solution.

Hugh Sidney, writing in *Time* magazine, describes George Washington's role at the Battle of Trenton as follows:

> Three columns were to have crossed the Delaware River; only Washington's made it across. The powder of his troops was soaked by a freezing rain, so they could not fire their arms. They had to defend with bayonets several times during the night. Washington's officers pleaded with him to call off the attack. The story goes that he stood on an old beehive in a muddy New Jersey field and turned aside every petition to retreat. The Battle of Trenton was won by the determination of one man.[1]

Brig. General Billy Mitchell also exemplified this important quality of leadership. At age thirty-nine Mitchell commanded a fighter squadron on the Eastern front in World War I. He strongly pushed for innovative ideas, such as forming large

99

. . . an invincible de-
termination can ac-
complish almost any-
thing . . .

Thomas Fuller

*The starting point of all
achievement is desire.*

Napoleon Hill

bomber armadas to destroy enemy formations and parachuting men and guns behind enemy lines. His ideas were so radical that it took great drive and persistence to convince superiors to try them.

Mitchell was most famous for his determined efforts to convince Congress and the War Department of the urgent need to spend more money on developing air power. He went to great lengths to do this, including making hundreds of speeches and writing numerous books and articles.[2]

Nelli Bly, the well known reporter for the *New York World* in the early 1900's, had a similar sense of urgency. Despite the warnings of friends and enemies, she could not be kept from investigating the graft and corruption that was found in high places in city government.

Another charismatic leader, Teddy Roosevelt, had one trait that over shadowed everything else: determination. As a child he was small, had poor eyesight and suffered from severe asthma. In his autobiography Roosevelt noted that he often lay in his bed struggling to breathe, afraid that he would not awaken in the morning. Weakened by his illness, he had to rely on Elliott, his younger brother, to shield him from the neighborhood bullies.

Nevertheless, Teddy willed himself to become strong both mentally and physically. Each day he pushed himself; he spent hours lifting weights and doing chin-ups. Interested in a wide variety of subjects, he read every book he could get his hands on. By the time he enrolled in Harvard, Roosevelt had become a man of extreme energy and enthusiasm. Faculty and students alike described him as being forceful and colorful.[3]

Numerous other people achieved unusual success in their lives by sheer force of their determination. Thomas Edison, probably the most prolific inventor ever, was once sent home from school because his teacher claimed he was too stupid to learn. R. H. Macy had seven retail failures before his store in New York became successful. In 1922, Harry Truman was thirty-eight, in debt and out of work. Twenty-three years later he was the leader of the free world. Finally, according to James C. Humes, author of a biography on Winston Churchill, "Few people realize that Churchill never could get into any university and had such a congenital lisp and stutter that doctors advised him against entering an occupation in which speaking was an important part.''[4] Later his voice would breathe hope into a frightened, discouraged country under siege.

All the determination in the world is of no avail unless you practice the fine art of **timing.** Knowing **when** to push for changes and improvements often determines the success of obtaining them. Most of us have heard the phrase: ''an idea whose time has come.'' People are not always psychologically ready to accept innovative ideas. Knowing when the time is right takes a degree of astuteness and patience.

In 1982 my staff and I at Federal Express developed recommendations for various types of sales incentive programs for our couriers. The objective was to inspire the couriers to increase their efforts to obtain new customers. For various reasons the proposals were turned down.

One morning about a year later Pete Willmott, the president of the company, came by my office. At the time we were experiencing a shortfall in revenue from the business plan. After saying hello he immediately said, ''You've just got to find a way to increase sales.'' ''Give us two weeks, and we'll have a solution,'' I replied. Realizing that Pete was ready to consider any reasonable approach, the best ideas from several earlier proposals were revised into a comprehensive, new plan. Two weeks later it was presented to him. The plan was approved and became the foundation of the very successful ''Breakthru'' courier revenue incentive programs at Federal Express.

The lesson: With determination and timing you cannot lose!

Genius is eternal patience.

> *Michelangelo*

To know how to wait is one of the great secrets of success.

> *James DeMaistre*

17

The Effective Leader Is Available and Visible To His or Her Staff

One of the problems of American corporations is the reluctance of managers to practice visible management — to get out and listen and talk to employees.

*Ed Carlson,
former
Chairman of
the Board,
United Airlines*

I always return from field visits with the feeling that I have learned something important.

One of the most important maxims of leadership is: **Be there with your personnel.** Sometimes that is difficult — especially when employees work on shifts. Even though keeping fourteen to sixteen hour schedules meeting employees on shifts is taxing, I have found it important to raising employee morale and to understanding the business.

The great lesson of leadership from the military is that the troops will put up with a difficult life, often with intolerable conditions, if their leaders do the same. History is full of examples of the impact of the commander's presence on the front lines:

- General Robert E. Lee made it a practice to visit the camp sites of his troops the night before each major battle. Often he would do this at the expense of getting sleep himself.
- General Patton was often seen riding the lead tank of his armor units. His daring and courage was an inspiration to his men.
- The Duke of Wellington, who defeated Napoleon at Waterloo, believed that Napoleon's presence on the battlefield was worth 40,000 soldiers.[1]

What applies in the military also applies to running a business. According to Thomas Peters and Robert H. Waterman, Jr., co-authors of *In Search of Excellence*, "management by wandering around," may be **the** most important thing managers can do to improve work quality and productivity. This involves frequently chatting with employees on-the-job to learn first-hand what is necessary to improve performance.

A feel for the subtleties of the business cannot be obtained by reading reports or financial statements. Rather, it requires direct and frequent input from employees at all levels.

Just wandering around is of little value unless you utilize the time to inspire and guide employees. This is accomplished by taking a sincere interest in each person. Your **attitude** is the key. It is demonstrated everyday by the dignity shown each person, the concern expressed for someone's personal problem and the appreciation given to those who give extra effort.

One of the major benefits of working with your people is that it enables you to detect and act upon negative employee attitudes before they spread and create morale problems. It is difficult for someone to continually disguise ill feelings toward the job or the organization. In one way or another the negative attitudes will be expressed with words and/or actions. Just the simple matter of how neat the work place is kept or how the equipment is treated tells a great deal about the extent of group pride and respect for the company.

Your role as leader is to determine the causes of negative employee attitudes and take early corrective action. Sometimes it is as simple as clearing up a misunderstanding or providing additional training. In other cases it may be necessary to do a better job of fulfilling an individual's needs for recognition or providing opportunities to perform more challenging assignments. Occasionally, it may be necessary to confront an individual directly and let him know that you will not tolerate his attitude. In short, you must quickly isolate the source of negativism and eliminate it. Otherwise, your department will never be a winner.

The extent to which you should include yourself in your operation depends on your level in the organization. If you are a first-level manager, you should spend at least 70% of your time with your people. Senior officers should devote at least a full day a week to making field visitations. The key is to maintain a regular pattern of listening and talking with the people who produce the product or deliver the service for your company.

When walking around an operation, you must be careful not to embarrass the manager in front of his or her subordinates by making comments about performance problems. The best approach is to keep your observations to yourself until you can

A desk is a dangerous place from which to watch the world.

John le Carré

103

arrange a private discussion with the manager.

Your primary mission during a plant or office visitation should be to get a feel for employee esprit de corps — the level of morale, pride and enthusiasm. This cannot be accomplished by a brief guided tour with you saying hello to employees as you walk past their work areas. Nor is it possible when accompanied by members of local management. Employees just will not be candid in front of their immediate bosses. A comprehensive visit takes at least several hours which should be divided between formal meetings and chatting privately with individuals.

Your secondary mission during a visitation should be to reinforce the company's quality values. A few words at the right time about the importance of having satisfied customers can have a powerful impact on employees when they are actually producing products or services.

Federal Express has a policy that requires an officer to visit each operating station a minimum of once a year. During such visitations he or she is expected to observe operations and conduct meetings with hourly personnel on all shifts.

Like radar, the good leader picks up obvious and not so obvious signals about conditions in an operation.

When conducting employee meetings, listen carefully to the type of questions asked. If most questions concern local conditions (such as vacation schedules or work assignments), it usually indicates that first-level management is not adequately taking care of employee needs. If the questions focus on broader matters (such as corporate plans or strategies), it could mean one of two things: either the employees concerns are being adequately addressed or they are so intimidated by local management that they are afraid to bring up their problems. If you sense that it is intimidation, you need to probe further in private conversations.

Sometimes you will encounter a shy group that will not ask questions or express their concerns. If so, try asking open-ended questions:

- What is preventing your team or section from being the best in the company? or
- What can we do to better support your efforts?

If you project a warm, friendly image when asking these questions, you will receive all the feedback you need.

Besides conducting employee meetings during plant or office

visitations, make it a practice to randomly select several people to talk to privately. Even a few one-on-one discussions can provide a good indication of the group's morale.

You know things are going well when the group's accomplishments are frequently mentioned. Look for what is said or not said about the group's manager. If nothing is said, dig deeper. Favorable, unsolicited comments given in private are a positive sign of high morale.

When holding such conversations, be careful to separate the wheat from the chaff — valued concerns or complaints from those that are not. Periodically, you will meet an employee with a bad attitude or one that can never be pleased. This is to be expected. What you are truly interested in is feedback from a number of people that, in total, paints an overall picture of a group's esprit de corps.

In summary, successful leaders always find time to make the rounds, chat with their people, show an interest in them and listen to their concerns and ideas. This is not just a nice thing to do; it is a necessity to achieve excellence in an organization.

V

The Three Key Requirements For Peak Leadership Performance

So far, I have discussed seventeen characteristics of effective leaders. Emulating these traits is a worthwhile strategy for anyone who wants to lead others successfully. Unfortunately, leadership entails more than acquiring isolated characteristics. Other conditions contribute to and sustain excellence over the long run.

Just as a flowering plant will fail to bloom year after year unless there are proper levels of sunlight, moisture and nutrients, so a person will not reach his leadership potential unless he:

- Is healthy or reasonably healthy,
- Has a satisfactory personal life and
- Is committed to life-long learning.

Certainly, one or more of these conditions can be absent from the leader's life for several months or even longer. All human beings have occasional health and personal problems; their motivation to learn also lapses. However, no one can consistently perform at his best if plagued by persistent ill-health or emotionally draining problems at home. This leads to a preoccupation with self, which interferes with one's ability to be empathic and involved with others.

A person can have the best health and personal life imaginable and still not achieve leadership success unless he is committed to life-long self-development. When personal growth and development ceases, leaders can become as obsolete as old machinery. Younger leaders with fresher knowledge and more refined skills replace them.

For organizations to thrive and flourish, management must always seek the best leadership available. Weaknesses or failures in leadership cannot be tolerated long. In time effective new leaders must be found.

In the following three chapters you will learn about specific actions you can take to unleash your full leadership potential. You will learn how to keep your health, build a fulfilling personal life and be a life-long learner.

VI

How To Keep Your Health By Managing Stress

From a recent survey of 9,000 workers from twenty-one companies and public service organizations a startling discovery was made. More than forty-five percent of the respondents said they suffered from burnout — a disabling reaction to job stress. According to Robert Golembiewski, who led the survey team, "These people were in pretty bad shape and felt high levels of emotional exhaustion."[1]

Leaders, particularly those on the way up in their organizations, are susceptible to high levels of stress. Not only do they have their own problems to worry about, but also those of their subordinates. Acting as a shepherd to others is emotionally draining. Different personalities have to be handled with sensitivity. Various personnel needs have to be addressed daily. Leaders are also faced with continuous pressure to produce favorable results. Finally, tension arises in constantly striving to get that next promotion.

Few tasks are more important to the leader than the effective management of stress. It is necessary for the leader to function effectively and to assist subordinates to do the same. Helping employees handle stress can yield substantial improvements in their job satisfaction and productivity.

This chapter provides insights into the nature of stress, how to spot it and how to manage it.

WHAT CAUSES STRESS?

When the mind perceives a situation as disagreeable, dan-

Every part of your body responds to your emotions. [2]

Robert E. Decker, Director, Palo Alto Center for Stress Related Disorders.

gerous or bad, it triggers the body's glands to release large quantities of the hormones cortisone and adrenalin. When these hormones are released, physiological changes occur, such as sharpened reflexes, heavy breathing, increased blood pressure and a more rigid heart rate. In effect, the body becomes mobilized for action and the threatened individual is able to react with increased strength and speed. This is called the "fight or flight syndrome." [3]

We experience many stress reactions each day. We rush to meet deadlines, we try to solve unexpected problems and we experience bad news.

Being human, many people worry about their jobs during the day and dream about them at night. They wake up tight and tense with less capacity to deal with new problems. This is the beginning of a vicious cycle leading to burnout.

From an analysis of the life styles of 1200 centenarians, it was concluded that the avoidance of stress was a common denominator of longevity.

When stressful conditions cause you to stay "hyped up" for prolonged periods and when the stress is not relieved, the body begins to deteriorate. Since the body functions as an integrated system, a breakdown will occur at the weakest link causing pain or illness. At this point your body is sending you a vital message: "Slow down, reduce your stress or else." If you heed the message and take appropriate action, your body, like a spring coil, will return to a normal condition. Failure to act could eventually result in serious illness.

OTHER IMPORTANT FACTS ABOUT STRESS

1. A **certain amount** of stress is important for life to have meaning. As an activation response, stress is a form of energy that is required for people to function effectively. Stress is necessary for us to have productive, happy lives. It keeps us on our toes, helps us forget minor physical irritations and provides a sense of exhilaration when we accomplish things in tight time frames. Without some stress, we become easily bored and lack direction. Often this is the problem of a newly retired executive. Suddenly, he or she does not have to make the effort each day to go to work and handle challenging assignments. Monotony from a purposeless existence can be as discomforting as a high level of stress.

The trick is to function with a level of stress that is life enhancing — not life threatening.

2. What causes stress is a highly individual matter. For example,

giving a performance appraisal is stressful to managers who dislike interacting with people. Other managers view appraisals as an opportunity to guide and help their subordinates. Losing an important promotion could cause one person to become despondent and another to redouble his efforts.

An individual's capacity for stress also varies. It depends on a number of factors including physical and emotional health, personality characteristics and past experience in handling stressful situations.

3. It is not the single stressful event that harms people, but long-term stress built up at increasingly higher, uninterrupted levels.

According to the American Medical Association, "80% of our diseases are either caused by or aggravated by stress."[4] These diseases range from minor ailments (e.g., aches and pains) to life-threatening diseases (e.g., strokes, heart attacks, ulcers and cancer). Stress can even weaken one's immune system.

Without stress resistance, the manager will change course to avoid problems, surrender to defeat, or dash himself to pieces.[5]

STRESS WARNING SIGNS

Some people become so accustomed to running their engines at full speed that they do not realize that their bodies are reacting adversely. They may ignore important warning signs manifested by a change in behavior, appearance, or physical sensation.

In his book *The Stress of Life,* Hans Selye identifies thirty-one stress warning signs. Some of the most common are:
- Migraine headaches.
- Exhaustion — even when getting adequate sleep.
- Irritability or impatience.
- Insomnia.
- Frequent constipation.
- Unusual numbers of colds, flu, etc.
- Restlessness — even at home.
- Rapid heart beat.
- Indigestion, stomach pains, backaches.
- Loss of appetite.
- Difficulty in concentrating — disjointed thinking.
- Neglect of physical appearance.
- Loss of optimism.

- Tendency to avoid or withdraw from difficult situations or problems.
- Feeling run-down or tired for long periods.

ENVIRONMENTAL CONDITIONS THAT COULD LEAD TO STRESS

In general, stress results from feelings of being pressured, of losing control over events and of being uncertain about the future. These feelings can occur in your private life or at work. Some of the more stressful situations include:

- Death or serious illness in the family.
- Divorce or separation.
- Unrealistic expectations about career success.
- Problems with children.
- Family conflict.
- Personal injury or illness.
- Constant pressure, both self-imposed and boss-imposed.
- Uncertainty over job security.
- Doing work which you do not like or are unsuited for.
- Pressure to compromise your principles for the sake of your career.
- Excessive change.
- Frequent travel over time zones.
- Being blocked from promotional opportunities.

WAYS TO PREVENT EXCESSIVE STRESS

A certain amount of stress is inevitable in our lives. There will always be some tension and conflict because of the imperfect nature of the universe we live in. Everything just does not run smoothly all the time. However, since an individual's reactions to stress are learned, they can be unlearned. In short, the effects of stress can be minimized by modifying habits and attitudes.

The first step in managing stress is to develop an awareness of being under excessive stress. Learn to recognize the warning signs previously presented. The short term stress reactions associated with tense events (such as giving speeches, confronting problem employees or making difficult decisions) are part of the job, but the continued feeling of pressure or tension that gradually builds up over time should, and can be avoided.

It is helpful to recognize which situations or events in your life cause you the most stress. (See previous lists.) If you are more aware of what causes stress and can recognize when you are under excessive stress, you will be better able to control it.

There are a number of specific strategies for managing stress. In general, they are centered around (a) gaining control over your life, (b) maintaining good health habits and (c) finding ways to release tension and enjoy yourself.

A. DEVELOP A SENSE OF CONTROL IN YOUR LIFE

Losing options is one of life's greatest stresses. [6]

The inability to have a high degree of autonomy in life leads to tension and stress. Autonomy means the freedom to pursue your own goals in life and to manage your affairs as you see fit. In the movie *Middle Age Crazy*, a father, who has just turned forty, begins to feel his life is controlled by others: his demanding sign installation business, a doting wife and relatives with personal problems. Unable to cope with all the strings tying him down, he angrily tells his wife, "I'm tired of being the daddy to everyone."

Emotionally healthy people maintain a high degree of control over what happens in their lives. They take the initiative and make things happen. They do not wait for good luck; they create it.

Emotionally stable people seem to have one more trait in common. They maintain a big picture perspective about life. They view the whole as good and decent and do not over react to the normal strains of daily living.

Some other suggestions for gaining better control of your life include:

Live today well; look to the morrow with vision and hope.

Bonnie Bailey

1. **Confront your problems head on** rather than avoiding them. Often you are better off to act and get things behind you than to procrastinate and stew about them. As William James says, "Nothing is so fatiguing as the eternal hanging on of an uncompleted task."

2. **Live in the present and look forward to the future.** Be at peace with yourself. Do not waste valuable time or energy worrying about what you could have done differently in the past. Nothing can be done about the yesterdays of your life.

117

Decide to be happy today, to make the best of what you have — your family, job, and friends.

Each morning when you awake try to start the day with a clean slate. Feel that you are free to act and do as you choose. You can choose to be cheerful, or you can choose to be sad. You can choose to be loving and caring, or you can choose to be hateful and selfish. **It is up to you!**

3. **Do not try to be all things to all people** by accepting every request to participate in volunteer work. A leader needs some time each day to unwind and enjoy family and friends. Attending too many civic and community functions at night just adds to stress. Instead, focus on a few volunteer projects that you enjoy.

4. **Think positive thoughts.** Try to do this in a number of different ways each day. First, make it a practice to look for the good qualities in people and then let them know how you feel about them. For example, if you encounter a store clerk or a restaurant waiter with a friendly, positive attitude, compliment him or her. If one of your work associates demonstrates a high level of determination in handling a difficult situation, express your admiration.

The second way to concentrate on the positive aspects of life is to periodically let your mind drift to an incident or occasion in the past that was particularly pleasant. For example, let good memories with your family be triggered by such stimuli as children playing baseball in a park, the aroma of a cake baking or a choir singing. Such images release pent-up tension by creating a feeling of warmth and love.

5. **Re-examine your life style** to determine if it is really worth the stress and tension that occurs from constantly striving to move up the management ladder. If you think money will eventually buy contentment, you are headed for a bitter disappointment. Money helps smooth the way, but it does not buy you friendships and the affection of your family. These are secured by taking the **time** to love and care.

Be realistic about your career possibilities. Everyone cannot be the head of their company. At some point in your life, you need to take stock of what you can realistically achieve.

If you look for the positive things in life, you'll find them.

Make money your God, and it will plague you like the devil.

Henry Fielding

Come to terms with yourself by setting a limit on what you are willing to do for job success.

Adopting a philosophy of doing the best you can and letting the chips fall as they may is necessary to avoid harmful stress. Isabel Moore expresses the same philosophy in a slightly different way: "Life is a one-way street. No matter how many detours you take, none of them leads back. And once you know and accept that, life becomes much simpler."

6. **Never use drugs or alcohol to help gain control in your life.** They make problems worse.

Therefore do not be anxious about tomorrow, for tomorrow will be anxious for itself. Let the day's own trouble be sufficient for the day.

Matthew 6:34

B. MAINTAIN GOOD HEALTH HABITS

Remember how you felt about your body when you were in high school or college? Chances are you were fifteen to twenty-five pounds lighter and in good shape. You felt good physically, and this influenced your entire attitude about life. According to Ralph LaForge, Managing Director of Preventive Medicine at the Sharp Memorial Hospital, "By initiating only one healthy behavior — exercise — you'll begin to change a whole gamut of additional healthy behaviors without even trying. You'll tend to eat better, sleep better, and take better care of yourself. And as a result, you'll also experience an improvement in your self-image."[7] All of these benefits of exercise help moderate stress.

Men in poor physical condition are four times more likely to die from a heart attack than those physically fit.

Dr. Lars Ekelund, Duke University Medical Center

Dr. Ralph S. Paffenbarger, Jr. of the Stanford School of Medicine says, "Exercise during middle age can actually retard physiological aging. Activity seems to lengthen life, maybe one or two years. We can expect that for every hour you're active, you will get to live that hour over — and possibly two more on top of that."[8]

One of the frequently heard excuses for not exercising is that "it just takes too long." Actually , medical tests indicate that it does not take much time to keep fit. Fifteen minutes a day of concentrated exercise has nearly the same training affect as an hour's workout.[9]

How does physical activity fight stress? Exercise burns off the hormones that produce stress.[10] Fifteen minutes of strenuous exercise can be more tranquilizing than strong drugs.[11]

Aerobic exercise (such as swimming, jogging, cycling and

brisk walking) are ideal ways to fight stress because they lead to sustained increases in heart rate and breathing without placing undue strain on the heart.

Considering the heavy time demands on leaders, the best approach is to workout five or six days a week for about fifteen to twenty minutes at a time. Exercise aerobically to get your pulse rate up continuously for this period.

Assuming you have the necessary self-discipline, it is relatively easy to establish an exercise routine at home. It is quite another matter to do so when traveling on business. Executives who travel spend most of their time attending meetings during the day and entertaining at night. The combination of inactivity, inadequate sleep and a propensity to eat rich foods has one result: poor health. With most evenings unavailable for exercise, one solution is to work out in the early morning by either jogging or using, if available, the hotel exercise room.

My routine for fighting the travel blah's is to eat a light dinner, preferably only fish and vegetables, and get up an hour early in the morning to jog. If it is too dark outside, I run in the hotel hallways. In effect, I trade off a little extra sleep for the good feeling and added stamina that comes from regular exercise.

If you want to adopt a regular physical fitness program, it is strongly recommended that you consult your physician **prior** to beginning. This is of particular importance if you are over forty years old.

There are several other rules about exercising that should be adhered to:

1. **Warm up prior to beginning strenuous exercise.** One of the best ways to do so is to perform a limited number of stretching exercises. There are several excellent books on the market that can tell you the best ways to stretch and thereby avoid pulling muscles.
2. **Start slowly and gradually work up to extended activity.** For example, if you decide to start jogging, your first two weeks should be devoted to jogging and walking.
3. **After exercising, take at least five minutes to slowly cool off.** This is the minimum time required to do so. People in a a hurry often forget this important advice by taking a cold shower immediately after exercising. They fail to realize that

People who exercise regularly do not experience significant disturbances in physical health and emotional well-being during periods of high stress.[12]

Jonathon D. Brown, PhD

their heart is already stressed by increased blood pressure and the production of a hormone called epinephrine that occurs when you cease vigorous activity. The cold shower can cause further stimulation of the heart resulting in a potentially dangerous condition.[13]

If you are not too tired, the best time to exercise is at the end of your work day. This is an excellent way to put the stress of the day behind you. It will also aid sleep. The one negative aspect of exercising in the evening is that it may stimulate your appetite. A heavy meal is not recommended because your body does not have sufficient time to burn off the calories.

One additional point about exercising: if you do not enjoy it and view it as just another chore, it could be harmful. According to Dr. Kenneth Greenspan, "Exercising while under stress can be dangerous because it puts an extra load on your heart."[14]

Other good health directives to follow include:
• Do not smoke,
• Keep your weight down and
• Minimize the amount of fat consumed in your diet. Fatty foods, such as meat, eggs, cheese and ice cream contain high levels of cholesterol. Overwhelming evidence supports the theory that cholesterol is an important factor in heart ailments and cancer. According to the National Center for Health Statistics, these illnesses account for nearly 50% of the deaths in the United States.

A recent study of 356,222 men age thirty-five to fifty-seven found that 80% had cholesterol levels over the recommended level of 200 milligrams per deciliter of blood and that the heart attack rate climbs sharply at the 220 level and above. The heart attack rate for the forty to forty-four age group with the 220 level was twice that for those with levels below 182. Dr. Jeremiah Stamler noted the importance of this discovery: "The claim is incorrect that excess risk does not start until the cholesterol reaches a markedly elevated level."[15]

According to the American Cancer Society, the best defense against cancer is to eat less fat and more fiber. Dr. Albert Mendeloff, a Johns Hopkins University gastrointestinal expert,

A man too busy to take care of his health is like a mechanic too busy to take care of his tools.

Spanish Proverb

recommends an intake of 30 to 60 grams per day of high fiber foods such as bran cereal, fresh vegetables and fruits. But do not go overboard on fiber, Mendeloff warns, because enormously high consumption of fiber may lead to excessive loss of some trace minerals.

A long-term, steady diet of foods containing beta carotene (i.e., carrots, tomatoes, spinach, asparagus and cantaloupe) is now considered helpful in inhibiting cancer. Vegetables like cabbage, broccoli, cauliflower and brussels sprouts produce similar effects.

4. **Keep regular sleep habits.** What counts is the regularity of sleep, not the amount. Altering sleeping patterns frequently creates the feeling of always being tired and lowers resistance to colds and flu.

Do you occasionally have problems falling asleep at night? If so, you are in good company as more than one-third of the population has insomnia from time to time. Studies show that missing several hours of normal sleep for a night or two does not affect your overall performance at work.[16] Although your judgment is not impaired, you may do poorly on routine tasks.

There are several effective techniques for overcoming insomnia. It is senseless to continue tossing and turning. Worrying about wakefulness only makes things worse. Instead, read a few chapters of a novel or get out of bed and perform some routine task such as straightening up your closet. Similarly, you can work on some aspect of a hobby that does not require a lot of thought.

Insomnia is most prevalent on Sunday night when most people are well-rested from the weekend. In "On Getting a Good Night's Sleep," Dr. Leonard Hayflick noted, "The shorter the time between waking up from one night's sleep and going to sleep again, the more difficult it will be to get to sleep." Since most people do not work on weekends, they sleep a couple of extra hours past their weekday alarm time. By Sunday night their body clocks are readjusted to a pattern different from that during the week.

If you maintain the same sleep patterns during the week and on the weekend, waking at the same time and avoiding a

Sunday afternoon nap, you can arrive at the office Monday morning fresh and ready to take on the events of the week.

5. **Eliminate using salt to flavor your food.** Today the average person consumes 20 to 50 times more sodium than the body needs. The excess is a significant contributor to high blood pressure — a silent life threatening disease that afflicts over 60 million Americans.[17] The processed foods we purchase are loaded with salt even though you might not taste it. For example, ''a half-cup of cottage cheese has as much sodium as thirty-two potato chips and a half-cup of chocolate pudding has more sodium than three slices of bacon. And one serving of canned soup contains 1000 milligrams of sodium — or nearly one-half the daily amount recommended for the average adult.''[18]

To reduce your intake of sodium, it is necessary to avoid salting your food at the table and cut back in the amount used in cooking. Wherever possible, substitute fresh vegetables and fruits for processed ones and minimize the consumption of salty snacks such as potato chips, crackers and nuts.

6. **Minimize your intake of caffeine loaded drinks like coffee, tea and colas.** Growing medical evidence suggests that excessive consumption of caffeine is a contributor to such diseases as ulcers and cancer. A recent study at Stanford University indicated that middle-aged men who consumed three or more cups of coffee a day had high levels of LDL cholesterol in their blood — the type that is linked to heart disease.[19]

The bottom line is that by modifying your smoking, eating and exercise habits, you substantially reduce the risk of getting cancer or suffering a fatal heart attack. Possibly the major payoff from maintaining good health habits is that you will experience the joy of being physically fit. With this good feeling comes increased stamina and enthusiasm — key ingredients for success as a leader.

One final note about maintaining good health habits — be careful that your pursuit of health does not become an obsession. You can become too puritanical and not enjoy life. As with everything, moderation is the key.

C. FIND WAYS TO RELEASE TENSION AND ENJOY YOURSELF

You need to reduce stress **both** at work and at home. No one can continuously perform at top speed when under excessive stress; it will eventually affect one's health. Your ability to achieve over the long-term is enhanced by adopting various coping strategies. Here are a few strategies that can be applied on the job:

1. **In everything you undertake give it your best**. I have never had regrets when I have done so. It is only when I did not properly prepare for a meeting or did not adequately address the issues in a report that I felt badly. Unquestionably, you feel your best when you do your best. Even making the effort will make you feel like a new person.

2. **Avoid the tendency to take on more than you can properly handle.** This is a particular problem for the small percentage of the population (approximately 15-20%) that are high achievers. Most leaders are in this category.

Build some slack into your work day.

To avoid burnout you should make a conscious decision to pace your days more evenly and to concentrate on only a few major areas or projects at a time. I would much rather have a staff member achieve major improvement in a limited number of areas rather than a little improvement in all of them. The idea is to get one or two items under control, then go on to two more. There is nothing more nerve racking than trying to do too much at once. I have actually seen it make people ill.

People rarely become stressed from tasks they enjoy and from which they receive satisfaction.

There is one exception to my recommendation of not overloading yourself with work. If your present job has become stressful, if it no longer provides sufficient challenge or rewards, it may be helpful to tackle a new assignment (such as a special project) that can be done after normal work hours. You may even want to turn a hobby into a part-time business. If this additional work is stimulating, it can actually reduce the stress you previously felt. Many people find such an approach energizing.

Excessive hours are not a problem if they contribute to your personal growth and a feeling that you are in control of your destiny. This is why many entrepreneurs can work day and night and with very little stress.

3. **Whenever possible relax during lunch.** Try to workout, take a walk, sit in the park, visit an art gallery or browse around a department store. One of my friends in the banking business makes it a practice to take a mid-day break to run five miles. He maintains that the workout eliminates built-up tension, thus enabling him to work long hours without getting tired. Whenever you need a break, eat lunch alone at a nearby restaurant. Get your mind off business by reading a book or magazine. When you return to the office you will feel great — ready to take on new challenges.

   Avoid regularly eating a hurried lunch in your office. Gulping down your food surrounded by all the problems and tensions of the day can be detrimental to your health. Some doctors claim that cholesterol levels increase by fifty percent when a person eats while under stress.[20]

4. **Take time to relax in your office.** Occasionally close your office door for a few minutes, have your secretary hold the phone calls and put your feet up. Let your mind wander away from business matters by visualizing a quiet, peaceful scene. Imagine a beautiful sunset in the mountains, a grassy wind-swept bluff or the silvery light of the moon upon a still lake. During such quiet periods the heart beat slows, and the blood pressure falls. The brain, which controls the body, refocuses from something unpleasant and stressful to something pleasant, and the body responds accordingly.

5. **Seek jobs that you enjoy.** Our time on earth is too short to constantly toil at things we really do not want to do. That does not mean that you should drop everything and go live on a tropical island. Yet, you should periodically evaluate whether you are devoting your work life to a goal that you feel good about or one that you will someday regret. Looking at your situation from this perspective is the first and most important step in making career decisions.

   In evaluating different careers and jobs I have found it smart to seek those that provide a measure of control over the planning **and** implementation of various tasks. Being able to complete something that you developed or designed provides a positive feeling of accomplishment. The more satisfying the work, the less stress involved.

6. **Try to view change as an opportunity to learn new things and develop yourself** rather than as a threat. Change can be exciting rather than stressful.

7. **Make "to do" lists.** Possibly the most effective stress management technique I have utilized over the years is to make lists of things I need to accomplish. I keep a list of "to do" items on my desk at work and another on my bedroom dresser. Once I place an item on a list, I feel freed of trying to remember it and worrying about it. Before I go to bed at night, I clear my mind by jotting down all the action items I can think of for the next day. This helps me have a restful sleep.

Leaders need to understand that not every problem has to be solved today, nor does every task have to be accomplished before you leave the office.

Over the years my efforts to clean everything up before I go home at night have led to considerable stress. Only recently have I learned that is is often more productive to stop work when I am tired and return to the office earlier than usual the next morning. When you are fresh, you can accomplish far more in a shorter time period.

Just as you need to manage stress at work, you need to do the same outside of work. The best way to do so is to learn how to **relax** and enjoy your free time.

Professor William Theobald of Purdue University has been researching the leisure patterns of executives for years. After surveying sixty chief executive officers he found that sixty percent of them did not normally take vacations. Of those who did, forty percent cut them short.[21] These figures substantiate the widely held belief that achievement-oriented people simply have a hard time letting down and relaxing. "These individuals tend to view leisure time as unproductive . . . They really don't enjoy it," says Prof. Theobald.[22]

Did you ever hear of someone on his death bed say: "I wish I'd spent more time at the office?"

As their careers reach the sunset phase, usually after age sixty, many hard-charging executives reach the conclusion that they have paid too steep a price for their success. Having lived in a pressure-cooker for so long, their health often fails prematurely. With high blood pressure or a heart ailment, they are unable to fully enjoy the fruits of their labors. Often I have heard such people say, "If only I had relaxed a little more along the way," or "If I just hadn't put myself under such strain all the time."

Fortunately, it is not too late to change your lifestyle. You can find a better **balance** between work and relaxation. You do not have to go to the other extreme and neglect your career. Continue working hard, but decide that your personal time is going to be more relaxing and enjoyable. Aristotle extolled the philosophy of living a balanced life when he observed that all vice stems from either an excess or a deficiency of a virtue.[23]

Half the battle in fighting stress is to have more fun in life.

There are many ways to relax and enjoy your time off. Here are a few that have been successfully used by business leaders:

1. **Devote twenty to thirty minutes a day to meditation and reflection.** Select a place where you can be alone. A peaceful, quiet setting is best. This time should be yours and yours alone without feeling a need to justify it to anyone. Let your mind roam at will. Think about the good things in your life — your loved ones and your dreams for the future. Come to terms with the mistakes you made. Be at peace with yourself, for you are a unique person with much to contribute to this world.

Be still and know!

   My preferred quiet time is the early morning. I usually spend a half hour or so observing the sun rise as I jog. What an uplifting way to begin the day!

2. **Develop some interests outside of business** to help you get your mind off work. The best way to do so is to be inquisitive about other matters. Make it a practice to notice new things each day whether it be in people, nature or the works of man. Besides enjoying the outdoors with all its fascinating colors and changes, I like to observe the construction of new buildings. To me, it is exciting to witness something permanent being created where there was nothing before.

Heighten your awareness of what is happening around you.

Working on hobbies is an excellent way to accomplish the objective of eliminating worry. Fishing, collecting stamps, playing golf or painting all accomplish the same thing: they keep your attention. Such activities, even though they can be quite demanding, seldom produce stress. This is because you elect to do them, and you can moderate your participation level.

Everyone needs a hobby outside of work that is totally immersing, rewarding and pleasurable. John Wanamaker, founder of the famous Philadelphia Department Store, said, "People who cannot find time for recreation are obligated sooner or later to find time for illness."

I could not tread these perilous paths in safety, if I did not keep a saving sense of humor.

Lord Nelson

3. **Develop a sense of humor.** Do not take yourself too seriously. Be able to poke fun at yourself and enjoy a good joke. In the intense world of the leader, humor plays an important role. First, it helps subordinates relate to their superiors and vice-versa. Second, humor relieves tension that may be impeding clear thinking. Many times I have seen a funny remark or joke made at an appropriate time in a meeting defuse an ugly debate or bring focus to an unproductive discussion. Finally, laughter is good for our emotional and physical health. In his book *Anatomy Of An Illness*, Norman Cousins goes further. He says that laughter helps to muster the energy needed to combat disease.

The sharing of a good joke with someone or laughing at life's absurdities can make almost any situation bearable. Humor, however, should never be at the expense of someone else. Racial, ethnic, religious or sexist jokes have no place in the life of a leader who cares about the dignity of others.

4. **Keep your mind on the pleasant aspects of life —** fond memories, the beauty around you, the joy of sharing and giving to others and the moments spent with loved ones. Try to forget the painful or ugly events of life that lead to stress. Instead, focus on what is good, what is right and what is beautiful.

Worry, not hard work, is what drains energy and vitality.

5. **Concentrate your energies on matters that you can have a positive influence on.** Many of us dissipate our energy by trying to change or improve things we have no control over. It is of little value to keep striving with all your might for some

unattainable degree of success. Well adjusted people are able to differentiate between the elements that they can control and those that they can not. They focus on achieving the possible.

Yesterday is experience, tomorrow is hope.[24]

6. **Maintain your self-confidence.** When you feel down or slightly depressed about a recent failure, stop and take stock of your past achievements. The realization that you have had major successes in the past and that the future is always open should help you regain your self-confidence. If you succeeded once, you can always do it again.

It is my observation that the true winners in life have something going for them beyond being at the right place at the right time: they view life from a long-term perspective. Winners fully expect to be successful eventually. There may be setbacks along the way, but they are merely short detours to be corrected and learned from.

7. **Do not try to be the "father of everything."** Many leaders I know place undue stress upon themselves by thinking that they have to be responsible for everything at work and at home. They also feel obligated to support important community and charitable activities with their leadership involvement.

Simplify your life!

When you feel overwhelmed by obligations, stop and sort out your "have to's" from your "choose to's." More often than not, you will find that you really do not have to do many things; you **choose** to do them. Begin the process of simplifying your life by saying "no" more often to demands on your personal time. Delegate more responsibility to your subordinates and family members. And finally, as much as possible, pay others to perform services for you, such as cutting the grass, raking the leaves and shoveling the snow. I have found that a simple, private lifestyle which centers around my family is necessary for regeneration of my "batteries."

Success goes to the person who recognizes that life is pretty much a percentage business.[25]

*Donald
Rumsfeld*

8. **Realize that you do not have to obtain perfection in everything you do.** Perfectionists are particularly prone to stress because they are easily disturbed if everything is not just right. They also tend to worry about how well they performed in the past. "If I had just done. . ." is a common statement from such people.

Learn to walk away from unfinished tasks that can wait until tomorrow. I will never forget working with my father-in-law, Don Harrison, fixing his farm fence in Hanover, Pennsylvania. One summer night at dusk we had nearly completed the repairs. I asked, "Do you want to keep going and finish the job?" His answer: "Let's go relax, it will be here tomorrow." Being able to occasionally say, "It will wait" or "So what" is necessary to avoid building undue pressure on yourself.

9. **Be playful. Lighten up. Have fun.** The normal person living to age 70 has 613,200 hours of life. This is too long a period not to have fun. Therefore enjoy the small pleasures of life. Periodically do something spontaneous that comes from your heart. The other day when my wife was on a business trip, I went out of my way to locate her car at the airport so I could put a note on the windshield telling her "I love you." You can send an unexpected gift to a spouse or friend, arrange a surprise birthday or anniversary party for a relative or take a box of doughnuts into the office for a morning coffee break.

10. **Find something bigger than yourself to believe in —** believe in God or promote a cause to benefit mankind. By doing so you are freed from the prison of focusing on your own problems and ailments. Dennis Waitley, author of *Seeds of Greatness,* suggests, "Call, visit, or write someone in need, every day of your life. Demonstrate your faith by passing it on to someone else."[26]

"For where your treasure is, there will your heart be also."

Matthew 6:21

There are many ways of managing stress both on and off the job. You need to figure out which of these suggestions are appropriate for you. **My best overall advice is not to take yourself or your career too seriously.** Give one-hundred percent plus at work, but leave ample time and energy for family and friends.

VII

Striving For A More Satisfying Personal Life

No man can deliver the goods if his heart is heavier than the load.

Frank Irving Fletcher

If your ambition in life is to reach your highest leadership potential, it is a definite advantage to have a supportive and happy personal life. With all the stress and strain leaders face each day, they cannot afford to be preoccupied with on-going, serious personal problems. A troubled marriage, serious financial difficulties and problems with children drain valuable emotional energy away from the all-out effort required to lead others successfully. On the other hand, a loving, supportive home environment can help you relax and refuel for the next challenge at work.

Obviously, everyone is going to have personal problems from time to time. The ability to cope with them is dependent on the individual's spiritual strength and the help and comfort obtained from friends and loved ones.

Having a satisfying personal life is a major determinant of long-term job success. The January 13, 1986, issue of *U.S. News and World Report* published the findings of a study of one million "ordinary millionaires" — those people who had principally made their fortunes on their own, not by inheritance. The article points out that the vast majority of them attribute much of their success to a stable and satisfying home life.

The purpose of this chapter is to assist you in maximizing your long-term leadership effectiveness by providing ideas and suggestions for ensuring a more satisfying personal life.

1. **Develop a well formulated statement of purpose or mission** in your life. Preoccupied with work and busy with their families, most people only have a vague idea of what they ultimately want in life. For years I too focused on short-term personal objectives (such as obtaining another degree or getting the next promotion). Several years ago all this changed when our church adult class participated in an unusual exercise. We were asked to spend fifteen quiet minutes visualizing what we wanted written as an epitaph on our tombstone. The exercise forced me to think of what I wanted to be remembered for after spending seventy to eighty years on earth. This was a difficult exercise because I had not given much thought to the true meaning of life or how I could contribute to making it better for others.

By reflecting upon what I valued most, I gradually developed the following mission statement for my life:

> To help others reach their highest leadership potential by sharing my knowledge, skills and philosophies through coaching, teaching, writing and by the example I set.

How up-lifting it was to decide on this mission and set out on the journey of fulfilling it!

Great men and women have a purpose or mission in life that is related in one form or another to **giving** themselves to others. Mohandas Ghandi, Albert Schweitzer, Mother Teresa, Martin Luther King and Madame Curie devoted their lives to eliminating suffering and improving living conditions for all people.

Success, therefore, should not be measured by one's power, status or fame. Rather, it should be measured by how much one gives of himself or herself to make this earth a little better for others. It is only when an individual's mission or purpose is focused outwardly on others, rather than inwardly on the self, that he or she can be at peace. **Success then becomes being at peace with yourself.**

Since your work and personal life change over time, you should periodically review your mission statement to determine if it accurately reflects your current desires for the future. It is possible that you will want to revise or change

If one advances confidently in the direction of his dreams, and endeavors to live the life which he has imagined, he will meet with success unexpected in common hours.

Henry David Thoreau

Cultivate optimism by committing yourself to a cause, a plan or a value system. You'll feel that you are growing in a meaningful direction which will help you rise above day-to-day setbacks. [1]

Dr. Robert Conroy, Associate Director, Menninger Memorial Hospital

your mission several times in your lifetime. What is appropriate at age twenty-five may not be as forty-five or sixty.

For your mission to become reality it must be accompanied by **specific goals.** The best time to establish personal goals is at the beginning of each new year. With the holidays behind you and most businesses in a lull, this is an excellent time to reflect on what you want to accomplish during the coming year.

2. **Add some variety to your life.** How easy it is to get into a comfortable routine of doing the same things, the same way, day after day! A certain amount of routine has its value, but routine can lead to boredom and complacency. The following United Technologies Corporation advertisement that appeared in the *Wall Street Journal* provides some sage advice.

Most people don't succeed in life because they don't know what they want to achieve in the first place.

"Get Out Of That Rut"

Oscar Wilde said,
"consistency is
the last refuge of
the unimaginative."
So stop getting up
at 6:05.
Get up at 5:06.
Walk a mile at dawn.
Find a new way
to drive to work.
Switch chores with
your spouse
next Saturday.
Buy a wok.
Study wildflowers.
Stay up alone all night.
Read to the blind.
Start counting
brown-eyed blondes
or blonds.
Subscribe to an
out-of-town paper.
Canoe at midnight.

135

Don't write to your
congressman,
take a whole scout
troop to see him.
Learn to speak
Italian.
Teach some kid
the thing you do best.
Listen to two hours of
uninterrupted Mozart.
Take up aerobic dancing.
Leap out of that rut.
Savor life.
Remember, we only
pass this way once.

Human beings, especially high achievers, are much like plants — every four or five years they need to be repotted or regenerated by taking on a significant new career challenge. This could be a promotion or a lateral transfer to a different position. If your present employer is unwilling to provide such opportunities and you are not prepared to go elsewhere, re-dedicate yourself to making the best of your present job. In addition, try to take on a challenging after-work activity in your community. Head a charity funds drive or become an officer in a civic or social club. Other people obtain self-actualization by turning a hobby into a part-time business or seeking a graduate degree.

Communicating frequently and intimately is the best prescription for a successful marriage.[2]

Dr. Howard Markman, Ph.D.

You should never stand still in life. Keep growing and developing!

3. **Seek a mate for life who is a buddy or a best friend —** someone to whom you can say, "I love you for what you are and how you make me feel." I am blessed in this situation with my wife Donna. We enjoy being together and care a great deal for each other.

To me, there are two critical requirements for a successful marriage. The first is that your **top priority** in terms of time and attention must go towards building and maintaining a strong relationship with your spouse. Everything else —

. . . A relationship is a living thing. It needs and benefits from the same attention to detail that an artist lavishes on his art.[3]

David Viscott

your children, career and hobbies — must be secondary. Second, there must be a high degree of mutual trust between the marriage partners. Being faithful to each other over the years is the foundation of this trust.

Donna Hulsizer, Ed.D., at Harvard University, adds two more ingredients for a successful marriage: both spouses should talk openly about their feelings, and the wife should have a substantial interest outside the home.[4] This provides self-esteem which is essential for a relationship to work.

One final thought about marriage — think of your relationship as a partnership in which you both share equally in the affairs of the home. This means that both partners should be willing to help with all household chores and caring for children.

4. **Take time to smell the daisies.** By this, I mean spend some time during your "helter skelter" career to sense and appreciate the beauty, emotions and excitement of the small things in life — such as quietly observing a robin feeding her young, walking in a snowy forest, watching children at play or participating in pleasant conversation with family or friends. To fully enjoy such pleasures you need to periodically slow down and open your heart and senses to what is occurring around you. Drink it in with the same gusto that you display at work.

Rabbi Alexander M. Schindler, President of the Union of American Hebrew Congregations, advises leaders to "never be too busy for the wonder and awe of life. Be reverent for each dawning day. Embrace each hour. Seize each golden moment."[5]

Enjoying the small pleasures of life is easier said than done for intense leaders who are used to a frantic pace, but it is vitally important that you do so before it is too late. In time your health will fail, and you will not have the ability to enjoy life as you may want to.

For the first few years after graduating from college, I was caught up in the typical syndrome of working nearly every waking hour. Had I known then what I know now, I would have tried harder to relax and spend more time with my family.

I was frequently away on business and chose to do office work evenings and weekends. Often I was too busy to go to

Carlyle was right when he said that this life is only a "gleam of light between two eternities." And still some folks take it so hectically and so seriously.

Amos Parrish

the beach with the kids or take them to the park. Thankfully, before it was too late, I realized what was happening and decided to make some changes in my life style. I quit bringing office work home unless it was absolutely necessary. I started making more time for my children; I attended their school events whenever possible and did things with them on the weekends. I made it a policy to never run an errand without some company. Each Saturday I took one of my sons or my daughter to lunch. I drove them to school. Occasionally, one of the children accompanied me on a business trip. These times together made me feel a part of their lives. Best of all, it provided many fond memories.

It took a while, but I finally realized what is truly important in life. It is **not** making more money, but loving those close to you and enjoying them while you can. As Henry Ward Beecher said, "No man can tell whether he is rich or poor by turning to his ledger. It is the heart that makes a man rich. He is rich according to **what he is,** not according to what he has."

Build your "memory bank" now before it is too late to make deposits.

Once in a while it is refreshing to take a personal day off to go to a ballgame, see your kids in a play at school or just relax at home. This does not mean that you stop working hard or reduce your regular office hours. Rather, it means taking a little time off now and then for the important people in your life.

It should be your personal policy to take all your allotted vacation time. In my career I have never seen anyone rewarded for skipping vacations. Leaders need periods of total rest to maintain their health, reflect on their lives and enjoy their families. Forgetting about work for an extended period has the added benefit of enabling the individual to return to work with renewed energy and creativity.

Skipping vacations could be a sign of insecurity. What is the individual afraid will be discovered during his absence? The leader's subordinates also need some breathing space — to occasionally be free of their boss. Vacations are good for everyone: the leader, his subordinates and the company.

5. **At home put building relationships ahead of task completion.** All their lives leaders have been trained to get out the work, to accomplish more and more. Often they carry this attitude home and become preoccupied with accomplishing lists of chores and fix-up projects evenings and weekends. Worse yet, they bring home a briefcase of paperwork to do each night.

Most leaders, to one degree or another, have overcommitment problems. The responsibility for running an organization just does not cease the moment you leave the office. Important reports and presentations have to be completed on time, no matter how long they take.

The solution to the challenge of balancing task completion with building relationships at home is not to simply say: "Stop bringing home your work." Instead, you should devise ways to clearly separate family time from work time when you **are** home.

Commitment is the single most important ingredient in making your family work. You must be committed to spending effort and time — at least as much as you spend on your career.[6]

Dr. Nick Stinnett

The most important family time is just before dinner, during dinner and after dinner. This two to three hour block of time should be dedicated to family time and family time alone. During this period do not even get **close** to your "to do" list or your briefcase. Instead, hang around your family. Become involved in what your spouse and kids did during the day. Be sensitive to their concerns and problems. If you must do the bills or office paperwork, do it after the children start their homework or after they go to bed. Better yet, devote the entire evening to the family and get up an hour earlier in the morning to work while the house is quiet. You can get more accomplished this way, and, best of all, you will not lose out on any precious family time.

6. **Keep in shape physically and mentally.** It is important to keep healthy; that is why I run several miles each day, eat the right foods and get plenty of rest. One of the things I enjoy most in life is rising early and jogging in the splendor of the morning sunrise. At that time I feel very close to God. When I return home, I feel like a totally different person. I am at peace with myself and feel an incredible lift in energy.

Your health must come first. Without it, you have nothing!

It is surprising how much more effective you can be on the job if you feel healthy. You are more alert and energetic.

Loving is the only sure road out of darkness, the only serum known that cures self-centeredness.

Ron McKuen

In my opinion there is one good way to destroy your career: heavy drinking. When you find that the only way to unwind after work is to have several drinks, you are headed for trouble.

7. **Give something of yourself to others.** There are many ways to do so, such as participating in charitable activities sponsored by churches, synagogues and civic organizations or taking an interest in someone in need and donating to worthy causes. The desire to make this world a little better for others is the primary reason that I have devoted so much personal time to writing this book.

8. **Do not risk more financially than you can afford to lose.** A man or woman preoccupied with risky investments is surely not going to have his or her mind on the job. The temptation is to seek the high returns normally associated with risky investments. Unfortunately, you always hear about the few who succeeded with this strategy but seldom about the many who failed.

Your policy should always be **never** to gamble the future of your family for the sake of making it big financially. Years ago Donna and I made the decision that we would first accrue sufficient funds for our children's educations before making any other investments. What peace of mind this has provided us over the years!

My investment strategy has three basic components. First, I always look for **quality** in investment opportunities. Investing in the best costs more initially, but it usually pays off with higher returns in the long-run. Second, I **diversify** my savings by investing in various types of financial and tanglible assets. Examples of financial assets include stocks, bonds and money market funds. Some of the most popular tangible assets are real estate and precious metals. By not putting all my eggs in one basket, I average out the effects of inflationary and deflationary periods.

The world is just too complicated, dynamic and changeable for one to be an expert in all matters that affect the value of investments. Even professional mutual funds managers **cannot** consistently outguess the direction of the markets. Individual

140

investors have even less chance to do so. Therefore, the best policy is to be a steady, long-term investor and keep diversified with a sizable percentage of savings in conservative investments.

The third part of my investment strategy is to seek a **reasonable,** not excessive rate of return from investments. I believe that financial success in most cases comes from not being greedy. Remember, all hogs eventually get slaughtered.

9. **Start early in your career to put away a little money from each paycheck** into an emergency fund or what I call a safety net. As with everything in life, your career is bound to have a number of peaks and valleys. Nothing is more depressing than absolute financial dependency on your employer; then you can never afford to quit or change careers. Your objective should be to save enough so that by the time you are at mid-career you can live for a year or two without a job.

Having a sizable nest-egg by your mid-forties is no longer a nice thing to do; it is a necessity. It is the middle-level management group dominated by people in their forties that is most susceptible to layoffs due to mergers, recessions and industry dislocations. In the past ten years over a million and a half middle-level managers have been displaced in the United States.[7]

The economic hardships on unemployed middle-aged people are severe. By age forty-five most couples have upscaled their standard of living by taking on substantial new debt to purchase larger homes and more expensive cars. On top of this, their children are just entering college, and their newly retired parents often need financial assistance.

As one displaced airline engineering manager bitterly told me, "After twenty-five years of dedicated service, I can't believe what happened. All of a sudden I'm dispensable. I always thought that if you worked hard and were loyal, that you'd be taken care of." Lulled into a feeling that his corporation would provide for him and his family for life, this man had failed to prepare for his rainy day.

The habit of saving is itself an education; it fosters every virtue, teaches self-denial and cultivates a sense of order.

T. T. Munger

Career job protection can no longer be guaranteed by any employer.

Besides the specter of increased layoffs for middle managers there is another development that makes life-long saving crucial: the trend toward reduction of retirement benefits by financially troubled corporations. This is something that never happened in the past. Only a few years ago, one could retire with the assurance that supplemental pay and health programs would continue until death.

The handwriting is on the wall! The paternalistic days of corporate America are gone forever. As a young person entering the business world today, you can no longer think of a forty to forty-five year career with a single company — even if you are an outstanding performer. A time span of ten to fifteen years is more realistic — if the company remains profitable. Otherwise your tenure could be even shorter.

Most young people in the work force live on thin margins. Often, dangerously in debt, they have no cushion available for an emergency and nothing saved for retirement. Even though they realize that Social Security will be unable to meet their retirement needs, they continue spending as if there were no tomorrow, hoping somehow that the future will take care of itself.

My advice to people in their 20's and 30's is to accumulate savings equal to one year's salary as soon as possible and thereafter save at least ten percent of all earnings. This level of savings should be sufficient to finance a comfortable retirement. If you wait until you are in the 40's to get started, you will have to double the savings rate to nearly twenty percent.

I do not know how many times my father told me that you can be more valuable to your company and sleep better at night if you have the confidence of knowing that you can quit. You do not want to be pressured into compromising your closely held beliefs for the sake of meeting house and car payments. Therefore, develop the habit of saving regularly. Sooner or later you'll be glad you did.

Only three out of every one hundred people reach retirement with a reasonable degree of financial security.

U.S. Dept. of Labor[8]

The doors are open to a better life! The future is open. It all depends on your attitude and outlook. You can choose to rush through life on the way to the grave, or you can choose to slow down a bit and take more time to enjoy your family and friends. You can choose to be grumpy, hard and dull, or you can choose to be happy, warm and interesting. The possibilities of making your life more loving, interesting and fulfilling are almost limitless.

Before you turn your attention to the concept of lifetime learning and how best to develop your leadership skills, I would like to leave you with a powerful thought about seeking happiness:

> Happiness can not be traveled to, owned, earned, worn or consumed. Happiness is the spiritual experience of living every minute with live, grace and gratitude.
> Dennis Waitley
> *Seeds of Greatness*

VIII

Leadership Skill Development
— A Lifetime Pursuit

Successful leaders recognize that developing leadership skills is a lifetime pursuit. In their study of ninety top leaders in all fields, Bennis and Nanus found, "It is the capacity to develop and improve their skills that distinguishes leaders from their followers."[1] The researchers also came to the conclusion that "leaders are perpetual learners."[2]

No matter what level you have achieved in an organization, you cannot afford to become static. All too often, executives reach a certain plateau in their organizations and then begin to coast. In a sense they become fat, dumb and happy. Simultaneously, their job responsibilities and scope of operations continue to grow, leaving them obsolete in terms of knowledge and skills.

Think of how enthusiastic and energetic you were to acquire new job knowledge when you first began your management career. More than likely, you were like a sponge — learning everything you could as quickly as possible. You probably took stacks of industry studies and trade journals home each night and studied them diligently.

If you truly want to reach your highest potential as a leader, it is imperative that you continue this almost child-like zest for learning throughout your career.

The extent of knowledge is doubling every two years. Soon, it will double in a year or less. When you feel that you have it made or that you know all there is to know, watch out — for it will not be long until you are replaced. In our competitive society there will always be people who are willing to make the necessary investments in time and energy to keep themselves up-to-date. Eventually, they will surface to the leadership positions.

At first the reader might think that being a lifetime learner must occur at the expense of having an enjoyable personal life. Quite the contrary, my wife and I consider learning an enjoyable hobby. We enjoy reading together, often sitting for hours studying and discussing topics and issues in the fields of management and education.

Years ago I decided that the normal reading of business periodicals was insufficient for my own growth and development. I wanted to develop as quickly as possible. What was needed was a series of learning experiences which involved a **commitment** on my part to others.

My first major developmental effort was to obtain an MBA degree at night and then to undertake an MS degree in finance. In both cases I had to request tuition aid approval from my boss and submit grades to him at the end of each semester. Next, I taught MBA courses part-time. Realizing that the students paid hard-earned dollars for the courses, I felt obligated to do the best teaching job possible. Several years later I began writing articles for management and training journals and taught leadership seminars at Federal Express. Writing this book has been my latest learning experience. All of these activities involved strong commitments on my part to people, thereby accelerating my development beyond what it would have been otherwise.

Contrast this type of commitment to one that you keep to yourself, say a resolution to learn more about leadership by reading a book a month. How many resolutions of this type are kept?

For maximum benefit and effectiveness, the commitments you make to grow and develop must be well thought out and organized. This requires that you:

1. **Develop a vision of where you want to be in your career five and ten years hence.** This vision should include the type of work you would like to do and the positions you would like to hold. The key is to select a functional area or part of the business that would be challenging and enjoyable. This could

Unless you try to do something beyond what you already mastered you will never grow.

Ronald Osborn

If you do not think about the future and prepare for it, you will not have one.

be operations, marketing, finance or whatever. The more specific your choice, the better. For example, in the marketing area your interest could be in sales, advertising, pricing or sales promotion.

There is something magnetic about people who obviously enjoy their work and know where they are going in life. Good feelings and positive energy radiate from such people.

2. **Identify the leadership skills and knowledge necessary for success in the positions of interest.**

Effective leaders are not satisfied with themselves. They have the courage to discover their shortcomings.

3. **Analyze your strengths and weaknesses** relative to the requirements of these positions. For example, if your goal is to someday become a product or division general manager, it would be advantageous to gain both sales and operations leadership experience early in your career. You may also want to polish your verbal presentation skills as they become increasingly important as you move up the management ladder.

Insights on your shortcomings can be gained by completing the *Self-Appraisal of Leadership Effectiveness* in the following chapter.

4. **Undertake leadership developmental activities that help overcome your weaknesses.** Several program suggestions are included in this chapter. Seek the advice and counsel of your manager in determining what to do. Besides making helpful recommendations, he or she may be of assistance in making arrangements for you to attend company sponsored courses.

Do not bite off more than you can chew. The acquisition of leadership skills takes time and does not occur overnight. If you try to do too much too fast, you may get discouraged. Chances are you will abandon your program before it does any good.

5. **Stick with your program.** It takes desire and extra effort to improve yourself. You must continually work at it. **Never** be satisfied that you know enough to get by.

Preparing for more leadership responsibility in advance does not mean that you should neglect your present duties in any way.

You must take responsibility for your own development.

Rather, it means you should continue giving one hundred percent and more. On the other hand, participate as well in one or two outside developmental activities on a **regular** basis. Here are a few suggestions:

1. **Attend college courses or seminars** that stress interpersonal relations and communications skills. These are the building blocks of leadership. An alternative would be to enroll in television correspondence courses which are offered by many universities.

2. **Assume a leadership role in a community organization.** This experience can provide valuable insights into how people function in groups and how they can be motivated.

Today a reader, tomorrow a leader.

W. Fusselman

3. **Read extensively.** Concentrate on material that broadens your leadership knowledge and sharpens your leadership skills. I have found that biographies are a rich source of insights into how to lead. Novels, with their imaginative plots, stimulate creative thinking and the consideration of new possibilities. Magazines like *Fortune* and *Success* also provide valuable leadership insights.

4. **Utilize the unproductive time spent in your car commuting to and from work and traveling between appointments by listening to audio tapes that help you develop leadership skills.**

5. **Become active in a leadership role with a professional or trade association.** This provides opportunities to practice leadership skills in a less threatening situation where you are not being evaluated by your employer.

Cultivate in yourself the qualities you admire most in others.

Arnold Glason

In addition to these off-the-job activities, you can prepare yourself at work for greater leadership responsibility. Study the techniques of successful leaders. Carefully observe how they articulate a vision of the future and how they inspire others to achieve it. Adopt the successful approaches with which you are comfortable.

You can also learn by watching weak leaders in action. Note how subordinates react to their leadership styles. Ask yourself if you would have used the same approach, and if not, what would you have done?

Another way to develop leadership skills on the job is to work on task forces dealing with specific problems in functional areas different from your own. This will broaden your horizons and expose you to the leadership styles of other executives.

The central thesis of Eugene Jenning's book, *Routes to the Executive Suite,* is that upward mobility in a corporation is primarily determined by acquiring and maintaining high visibility and exposure. To me, developing and maintaining good relationships with peers and subordinates is equally important. The best way to do so is to unselfishly offer them help and assistance.

Be careful, however, not to become so involved in extracurricular task forces that your normal duties slip. Most promotions are awarded to those that please their immediate bosses by performing in an outstanding manner. **Your track record is what is important.**

The best way to become involved in a corporate task force is to be recommended for the assignment. No boss will make such a recommendation unless you have earned it by exceeding your goals and by having a good working relationship with him or her.

Finally, one of the best ways to develop leadership skills is to share your knowledge and experiences with younger managers. As in any type of coaching role, the coach benefits as much as the trainee.

The advantages of a self-development program are threefold. First, and most important, to grow and develop is stimulating and exciting. The thrill of living is stretching out beyond what one thinks possible — constantly improving — becoming someone you are not yet today. The realization that you are growing and developing is a powerful personal motivator giving you a different outlook on life — an uplifting of spirits that enables you to better cope with the unpleasant aspects of work and personal problems. The daily nuisances of life do not appear so great when you are dealing on the higher plane of self-development. Second, the leadership skills and knowledge acquired from your self-development efforts will improve your qualifications for promotion. Third, when that promotion does come, you will be in a much better position to succeed than if you did nothing until the opportunity came your way. You will already have developed

None of the secrets of success will work unless you do.

Have the daring to accept yourself as a bundle of possibilities and undertake the game of making the most of your best.

Henry Emerson Fosdick

many of the leadership abilities necessary for success in the new job.

It is easy to get into the comfortable rut of continually doing your job in the same old manner but then suddenly realize that you are being passed up for promotions. The best way to keep this from happening is to perform in an outstanding manner and become committed to a **continuous** program of self-improvement, both on and off the job. It is not so much how intensive your developmental efforts are at one time, but the fact that you regularly work at it over extended periods.

Great things are not done by impulse but by a series of small things brought together.

*Vincent
Van Gogh*

If the idea of lifetime learning appears a bit overwhelming at this point in your career, remember the answer to the question: how does one go about eating an elephant? **One bite at a time!** The acquisition of vintage leadership skill is much like Vince Lombardi's definition of football: "a game of inches." The Chinese have another way of saying the same thing: "A journey of a thousand miles begins with a single step." So approach the future with a vision in your mind of what you want to be, think of it often, and steadily, ever so steadily, work to make it happen by taking one small developmental step at a time. You will succeed if you approach your career in this fashion.

IX

Appraising Your Leadership Effectiveness And Planning For Improvement

*To become what we are
capable of becoming is
the only end of life.*

Spinoza

Art Bass, the former President of Federal Express and Chairman of Midway Airlines once told me, "Everyone is like a round dowel with a flat side." In other words, everyone has weaknesses. The beautiful thing about life is that with all our flaws and flat sides, we can still aspire to any height **if** we are willing to invest the time and energy to do so.

To improve your leadership performance, you first need to learn more about yourself — your strengths and weaknesses. Eric Hoffer said it best: "To become different from what we are, we must have some awareness of what we are."

You can obtain a comprehensive picture of your leadership capability by **honestly** answering the questions on the following pages. Do not be discouraged by the number of them. They are all important. To obtain the maximum benefit from the exercise, I recommend that you complete a few pages each night for about a week. Reflect on each question before marking an answer. You will then be ready to proceed with the developmental steps presented at the end of this chapter.

SELF APPRAISAL OF LEADERSHIP EFFECTIVENESS

	ALWAYS	USUALLY	SOMETIMES	RARELY	IDEAS OR ACTIONS TO IMPROVE (NOTES)
1. Do you lead from power or your interpersonnel skills?					
2. Do you put the needs of your subordinates above your own?					
3. Do you visualize or identify what is necessary for the long-term success of your organization?					
4. Do you communicate a vision of the future to your personnel?					
5. Do you regularly involve your direct subordinates in planning for the future?					
6. Do you encourage and inspire everyone to give his or her best?					
7. Do you assist employees in satisfying their work related needs?					

156

ALWAYS USUALLY SOMETIMES RARELY

IDEAS OR ACTIONS
TO IMPROVE
(NOTES)

8. Do you "go to bat" for your people with upper management?

9. Do you hold people accountable for their actions?

10. Do you treat everyone in a fair but firm manner?

11. Do you set challenging but realistic performance standards?

12. Do you expect and insist on excellence?

13. Do you present a bearing that indicates you are in command?

14. Do you take disciplinary action against those who fail to measure up?

ALWAYS   USUALLY   SOMETIMES   RARELY

IDEAS OR ACTIONS
TO IMPROVE
(NOTES)

15. Do you keep your word?

16. Do you have the courage to:
    - Handle defeat gracefully?
    - Face conflict head on?
    - Bear your burdens?

17. Do you give credit to those who make worthwhile suggestions?

18. Do you trust your people until proven otherwise?

19. Do you bring out the best in your employees by showing confidence in them?

20. Do you maintain a sense of humor?

21. Do you continually seek new and better ways to reach your organization's goals?

ALWAYS USUALLY SOMETIMES RARELY

*IDEAS OR ACTIONS
TO IMPROVE
(NOTES)*

22. Do you provide abundant performance feedback to all your people?

23. Do you openly demonstrate appreciation for their efforts?

24. Do you keep the confidence of employees who confide in you?

25. Do you give your people the freedom to express opinions that might be different from yours?

26. Do you recognize the achievements of your personnel?

27. Do you emphasize key company philosophies of how employees should be treated?

28. Do you give high priority to resolving employee problems and complaints?

ALWAYS USUALLY SOMETIMES RARELY

IDEAS OR ACTIONS
TO IMPROVE
(NOTES)

29. Do you share information openly and willingly?

30. Do you let subordinates know what is expected of them?

31. Do you act on performance violations immediately?

32. Do you take time to explain the reason(s) for changes?

33. Do you encourage ideas and suggestions?

34. Do you strive to develop an organizational climate that encourages open and free exchange of information?

35. Do you put directives in the form of a request rather than a demand?

	ALWAYS	USUALLY	SOMETIMES	RARELY	IDEAS OR ACTIONS TO IMPROVE (NOTES)
36. Do you involve your personnel in decision-making?					
37. Do you listen carefully?					
38. Do you encourage subordinates to think on their own?					
39. Do you explain the reason(s) why you have to reject impractical ideas?					
40. Do you assume responsibility for the actions of your employees?					
41. Do you try to instill in your work force the desire to be the best — number one?					
42. Do you actively seek promotional opportunities for your outstanding performers?					

	ALWAYS	USUALLY	SOMETIMES	RARELY	IDEAS OR ACTIONS TO IMPROVE (NOTES)
43. Do you regularly spend time with your people?					
44. Do you maintain a questioning attitude toward everything done in your department?					
45. Do you keep a satisfactory balance between your job and your home life?					
46. Do you take time to enjoy the small but pleasant things in life?					
47. Do you maintain a positive mental attitude?					
48. Do you keep in shape physically?					
49. Do you regularly save for the future?					

	ALWAYS	USUALLY	SOMETIMES	RARELY	IDEAS OR ACTIONS TO IMPROVE (NOTES)
50. Do you inform superiors of the favorable things your people do?					
51. Do you try to anticipate what **could** go wrong in your operation?					
52. Do you take action in advance to prevent possible problems?					
53. Do you remain calm during crises?					
54. Do you make difficult decisions without procrastination?					
55. Do you let people perform in their own style?					
56. Do you concentrate on the areas of your job that have the highest payoff?					

	ALWAYS	USUALLY	SOMETIMES	RARELY	IDEAS OR ACTIONS TO IMPROVE (NOTES)
57. Do you delegate as much as possible?					
58. Do you set weekly and daily priorities of what you want to accomplish?					
59. Do you establish deadlines for yourself?					
60. Do you show concern for your employees by ensuring that the work place is clean, safe and comfortable?					
61. Do you maintain an open mind when a superior questions something about your operation?					
62. Do you point out areas to subordinates that need improvement?					
63. Do you maintain a sense of urgency for getting important things done promptly and effectively?					

ALWAYS USUALLY SOMETIMES RARELY

IDEAS OR ACTIONS
TO IMPROVE
(NOTES)

64. Do you control your temper?

65. Do you keep your mind open to new ideas?

66. Do you show respect and courtesy to your peers?

67. Do you go out of your way to work as a team member?

68. Do you accept constructive criticism gracefully?

69. Do you encourage your subordinates to assume greater responsibility for doing their jobs better?

70. Do you assume the blame when you make a mistake?

	ALWAYS	USUALLY	SOMETIMES	RARELY	IDEAS OR ACTIONS TO IMPROVE (NOTES)
71. Do you treat your subordinates with respect and dignity?					
72. Do you work hard at clearing away the obstacles that hinder the performance of your personnel?					
73. Do you evenly enforce important rules and regulations?					
74. Do you demonstrate total commitment to doing the best job possible?					
75. Do you make yourself available to everyone, not just those you like or respect?					
76. Do you give individuals opportunities to develop and implement their own ideas?					
77. Do you provide opportunities for someone to learn your job?					

	ALWAYS	USUALLY	SOMETIMES	RARELY	IDEAS OR ACTIONS TO IMPROVE (NOTES)
78. Do you introduce new company policies as if they were your own rather than something imposed on you?					
79. Are you tactful when saying "no"?					
80. Do you actively coach your employees?					
81. Do you willingly accept change?					
82. Do you admit it when you make a mistake or do not have an answer?					
83. Do you maintain good health habits?					
84. Do you strive to remember the names of people in your department?					

	ALWAYS	USUALLY	SOMETIMES	RARELY	IDEAS OR ACTIONS TO IMPROVE (NOTES)
85. Do you maintain a cheerful, pleasant attitude?					
86. Do you spend personal time developing yourself for the future?					

After answering all the questions, go back over your responses to identify those marked "always" and "rarely." Your leadership strengths are identified by your "always" answers. This knowledge is important because **successful leaders build on their strengths.** They seek positions where they know they can shine.

This important strategy can be limiting if you have serious weaknesses that are not corrected or minimized—for example the inability to get along with colleagues or to plan ahead for the future. The people who continually advance in their companies are those that leverage their strengths and never stop trying to overcome their deficiencies.

With this in mind, review the questions answered "rarely." These areas require work. Use the space on the right hand side of each page to jot down ideas on how to improve. For example, if you infrequently involve your direct subordinates in planning for the future (question #5), you may decide to improve by holding quarterly planning meetings.

After thinking about all the questions marked "rarely," rank them according to the priority of importance to your career. Then employing the philosophy of taking one step or bite at a time, develop and implement your improvement program. As you do so, carefully monitor the results and reactions of subordinates and peers. Obtain their feedback. If the early results are positive, continue in the direction that you are headed. Negative feedback should be evaluated to determine where you went wrong.

As you work toward improving your leadership skills, do not expect success overnight. Be patient with yourself; it takes time to transform a new way of behaving into a comfortable habit. Subordinates also need time to adjust to changes in the boss's style. At first, they may be suspicious. As you demonstrate consistency over time, they will respond favorably with comments such as, "The boss has sure changed for the better."

The fruits of your self-development labors will be many. Besides opening up salary advancement and promotional opportunities, you will gain a sense of accomplishment by becoming a more competent leader. Your esteem in the organization will grow. Above all, you will have improved your capacity to participate in one of life's richest experiences — helping others reach their highest potential. The lives of your employers and associates will be better for having known you.

X

Other Inspiring Quotations On Leadership Attributes And Ideals Worth Emulating

One of the great joys of life is discovering new insights into human nature in general and yourself in particular. From the observations of poets, statesmen, writers and business executives comes a wealth of wisdom that provides understanding, guidance and inspiration for leaders or potential leaders in all walks of life.

In this section of the book you will learn from the likes of Churchill, Emerson, Schweitzer, Franklin, Iacocca, Edison, Lincoln, Twain, Peale and many others. You will find that their words speak to you or have relevance for you in different ways as conditions and situations change in your life. At one time, a saying may lead you to discover an important truth about yourself, strengthen a conviction or reinforce an important value. At another time, the words may inspire you to take action in an area where you had not previously planned to do so.

Hence, refer often to the treasury of quotations found on the following pages and throughout the book. Memorize those that are most meaningful to you. Most of all, enjoy the feelings expressed. For as William Ellery Channing tells us:

> Quotations are true levelers. They give to all who
> will faithfully use them the spiritual presence of the
> best and greatest of the human race.

Ideals are like stars. You will not succeed in touching them with your hands. But like the seafaring man on the desert of waters, you choose them as your guides, and following them you will reach your destiny.
Carl Schurz

Aim at the sun, and you may not reach it; but your arrow will fly far higher than if you aimed at an object on a level with yourself.
J. Howse

Finish each day and be done with it . . . you have done what you could; some blunders and absurdities no doubt crept in; forget them as soon as you can. Tomorrow is a new day; you shall begin it well and serenely.
Ralph Waldo Emerson

The gem cannot be polished without friction, nor man perfected without trials.
Chinese Proverb

One man can completely change the character of a country, and the industry of its people, by dropping a single seed in fertile soil.
John C. Gifford

I don't know what your destiny will be, but one thing I know: the only ones among you who will be really happy are those who will have sought and found how to serve.
Dr. Albert Schweitzer

If you think you can, or you think you can't, you're probably right.
Mark Twain

Any man who is honest, fair, tolerant, kindly, charitable of others and well behaved is a success, no matter what his station in life.
Jay E. House

Faith without works is like a bird without wings; though she may hop about on earth, she will never fly to heaven. But when both are joined together, then doth the soul mount up to her eternal rest.
Beaumont

A leader is best when people barely know he exists . . . when his work is done, his aim fulfilled, they will say, we did this ourselves.
Lao-Tse

Three men were laying brick.
The first was asked, "What are you doing?"
He answered, "Laying some brick."
The second man was asked, "What are you working for?"
He answered, "Five dollars a day."
The third man was asked, "What are you doing?"
He answered, "I am helping to build a great Cathedral."
Which man are you?
Charles Schwab

Character is the foundation stone upon which one must build to win respect. Just as no worthy building can be erected on a weak foundation, so no lasting reputation worthy of respect can be built on a weak character. Without character, all effort to attain dignity is superficial, and results are sure to be disappointing.
R. C. Samsel

No one ever finds life worth living — he has to make it worth living.
Author Unknown

Techniques don't produce quality products or pick up the garbage on time; people do, people who care, people who are treated as creatively contributing adults.
    Tom Peters

Real joy comes not from ease or riches or from the praise of men, but from doing something worthwhile.
    Sir Wilfred Grenfell

The law of harvest is to reap more than you sow. Sow an act, and you reap a habit; sow a habit, and you reap a character; sow a character and you reap a destiny.
    G. D. Boardman

The man who lives for himself is a failure; the man who lives for others has achieved true success.
    Norman Vincent Peale

Happiness is a by-product of an effort to make someone else happy.
    Greta Palmer

Every worthwhile accomplishment, big or little, has its stages of drudgery and triumph; a beginning, a struggle, and a victory.
    Anonymous

I know the price of success — dedication, hard work and unremitting devotion to the things you want to see happen.
    Frank Lloyd Wright

Nearly all men can stand adversity, but if you want to test a man's character, give him power.
  Abraham Lincoln

Difficulties mastered are opportunities won.
  Winston Churchill

The world stands aside to let anyone pass who knows where he is going.
  David Starr Gordon

He who is false to the present duty breaks a thread in the loom, and you will see the effect when the weaving of a lifetime is unraveled.
  Ellery Channing

If you can give your son only one gift, let it be enthusiasm.
  Bruce Barton

There is no road too long to the man who advances deliberately and without undue haste; no honors too distant to the man who prepares himself for them with patience.
  Bruyers

Happiness comes of the capacity to feel deeply, to enjoy simply, to think freely, to risk life, to be needed.
  Storm Jameson

I've felt that dissatisfaction is the basis of progress. When we become satisfied in business we become obsolete.
  J. W. "Bill" Marriott, Sr.

Show me a man that you honor, and I will know what kind of a man you are, for it shows me what your ideal of manhood is, and what kind of a man you long to be.
    Thomas Carlyle

Plant the seeds of expectation in your mind; cultivate thoughts that anticipate achievement. Believe in yourself as being capable of overcoming all obstacles and weaknesses.
    Norman Vincent Peale

Whether our efforts are, or are not, favored by life, let us be able to say, when we come near the great goal, I have done what I could.
    Louis Pasteur

If there be any truer measure of a man than by what he does, it must be what he gives.
    Robert South

Read every day something no one else is reading. Think every day something no one else is thinking. It is bad for the mind to be always a part of unanimity.
    Christopher Morley

I believe the first test of a truly great man is humility.
    John Ruskin

Those who have not sown anything during their responsible life will have nothing to reap in the future.
    George Gurdjieff

It is better to create than to be learned; creating is the true essence of life.
    Niebuhr

Nothing is impossible to a willing heart.
    John Heywood

By constant self-discipline and self-control you can develop greatness of character.
    Grenville Kleiser

The man who has accomplished all that he thinks worthwhile has begun to die.
    E.T. Trigg

Progress results from persistence with purpose.
    Frank Tyger

To do something, however small, to make others happier and better is the highest ambition, the most elevating hope, which can inspire a human being.
    John Lubbock

Many of the greatest men have owed their success to industry rather than cleverness.
    John Lubbock

Without perserverence, talent is a barren bed.
    Welsh Proverb

Faith in the ability of a leader is of slight service unless it be united with faith in his justice.
George B. Goethals

There is one element that is worth its weight in gold and that is loyalty. It will cover a multitude of weaknesses.
Philip Armour

We grow great by dreams.
Woodrow Wilson

Life can only be understood backward, but it must be lived forward.
Niels Bohr

Failure should challenge us to new heights of accomplishment, not pull us to new depths of despair. Failure is delay, but not defeat. It is a temporary detour, not a dead-end street.
William Arthur Ward

It's an old adage that the way to be safe is never to be secure. Each of us requires the spur of insecurity to force us to do our best.
Harold W. Dobbs

Ideas go booming through the world louder than cannons. Thoughts are mightier than armies. Principles have achieved more victories than horsemen or chariots.
W.M. Paxton

Great necessity elevates man, petty necessity casts him down.
Goethe

You are already of consequence in the world if you are known as a man of strict integrity.
Grenville Kleiser

Any man worth his salt will stick up for what he believes right, but it takes a slightly bigger man to acknowledge instantly and without reservation that he is in error.
Gen. Peyton C. March

Half of the world is on the wrong scent in the pursuit of happiness. They think it consists in having and getting, and in being served by others. It consists in giving and serving others.
Henry Drummond

He who cherishes a beautiful vision, a lofty ideal in his heart, will one day realize it.
James Allen

Live your life each day as you would climb a mountain. An occasional glance toward the summit keeps the goal in mind, but many beautiful scenes are to be observed from each new vantage point. Climb slowly, steadily, enjoying each passing moment, and the view from the summit will serve as a fitting climax for the journey.
Harold V. Melchert

Who dares nothing, need hope for nothing.
Johann Schiller

Ideas control the world.
James A. Garfield

The real difference between men is energy. A strong will, a settled purpose, an invincible determination can accomplish almost anything, and in this lies the distinction between great men and little men.
Thomas Fuller

Pride is at the bottom of all great mistakes.
John Ruskin

When people are made to feel secure and important and appreciated, it will no longer be necessary for them to whittle down others in order to seem bigger in comparison.
Virginia Arcastle

If you play it safe in life, you've decided that you don't want to grow anymore.
Shirley Hufstedler

We're worn into grooves by time — by our habits. In the end, these grooves are going to show whether we've been second rate or champions.
Frank B. Gilberth

What a man does for others, not what they do for him, gives him immortality.
Daniel Webster

There is nothing in the world so much admired as a man who knows how to bear unhappiness with courage.
Seneca

Half of the harm that is done in this world is due to people who want to feel important . . . they do not mean to do harm . . . they are absorbed in the endless struggle to think well of themselves.
T. S. Eliot

Success is not due to a fortuitous concourse of stars at our birth, but to a steady trial of sparks from the grindstone of hard work each day.
Kenneth Hildebrand

Take the course opposite to custom and you will almost always do well.
Jean Jacques Rousseau

As a man grows older . . .
  . . . He values the voice of experience more and the voice of prophecy less.
  . . . He finds more of life's wealth in the common pleasures — home, health and children.
  . . . He thinks more about the work of men and less about their wealth.
  . . . He begins to appreciate his own father a little more.
  . . . He hurries less, and usually makes more progress.
  . . . He esteems the friendship of God a little higher.
Roy L. Smith

The four-way test of the things we think, say or do:
  . . . Is it the truth?
  . . . Is it fair to all concerned?
  . . . Will it build good will and better relationships?
  . . . Will it be beneficial to all concerned?
Rotary International Motto

He who wishes to fulfill his mission in the world must be a man of one idea, that is, of one great overmastering purpose, overshadowing all his aims, and guiding and controlling his entire life.

Bate

When a man realizes his littleness his greatness can appear.

H. G. Wells

The rung of a ladder was never meant to rest upon, but only to hold a man's foot long enough to enable him to put the other somewhat higher.

Thomas Huxley

If a man lives a decent life and does his work fairly and squarely so that those dependent upon him and attached to him are better for his having lived, then he is a success.

Teddy Roosevelt

Do not waste a minute — not a second — in trying to demonstrate to others the merits of your performance. If your work does not indicate itself, you cannot vindicate it.

Thomas W. Higginson

Prosperity is a great teacher; adversity a greater.

William Haylitt

Any man can work when every stroke of his hand brings down the fruit rattling from the tree to the ground; but to labor in season and out of season, under every discouragement, by the power of truth — that requires a heroism which is transcendent.

Henry Ward Beecher

A really great man is known by three signs — generosity in the design, humanity in the execution, moderation in success.
  Bismark

You can buy a man's time, you can even buy his physical presence at a given place, but you cannot buy enthusiasm . . . you cannot buy loyalty. . . you cannot buy the devotion of hearts, minds, or souls. You must earn these.
  Charles Frances

Every man has a right to his opinions, but no man has a right to be wrong in his facts.
  Bernard M. Baruch

No man can really be big who does not read widely outside his own field.
  Theodore N. Vail

There's no gain without pain.
  Benjamin Franklin

If you will call your troubles experiences, and remember that every experience develops some latent force within you, you will grow vigorous and happy, however adverse your circumstances may seem to be.
  John R. Miller

The speed of the boss is the speed of the team.
  Lee Iacocca

Riches without charity are nothing worth. They are a blessing only to him who makes them a blessing to others.
    Henry Fielding

Success is where preparation and opportunity meet.
    Bobby Unser

There is no fire like passion, there is no shark like hatred, there is no snare like folly, there is no torrent like greed.
    Buddha

It is only when you are pursued that you become swift.
    Kahil Gibran

A father can do nothing better for his children than to love their mother.
    Author Unknown

Thank God — every morning when you get up — that you have something to do which must be done, whether you like it or not. Being forced to work, and forced to do your best, will breed in you a hundred virtues which the idle never know.
    Charles Kingsley

It's no exaggeration to say that a strong positive self-image is the best possible preparation for success in life.
    Dr. Joyce Brothers

As the essence of courage is to stake one's life on a possibility, so the essence of faith is to believe that the possibility exists.
    William Salter

Of those to whom much is given, much is required.
> J. F. Kennedy

Love is the most important ingredient for success. Without it, your life echoes emptiness. With it, your life vibrates warmth and meaning.
> *The Best of Success*

Life is a two-stage rocket. The first is physical energy — it ignites, and we are off. As physical energy diminishes, the spiritual stage must ignite to boost us into orbit, or we will fall back or plateau.
> W. F. Smith

RESOLUTION

Whereas the Supreme Power of the universe has deemed it natural to create human beings of various colors, races, and creeds; and

Whereas in his sight they all are his equally beloved children;

Therefore be it resolved that there is no superior race or group of peoples and that all men are brothers of equal rank; and be it further resolved that we know this and believe it now and forever!
> W. Newman

XI

Encouragement For Leaders
Or Aspiring Leaders

With so much involved in effectively leading others, **is it all really possible?** It is my unshakable belief, born from years of leading and studying leaders, that any person endowed with intelligence and who likes people can rise to the highest levels of an organization. Sadly, most people tap into only eight or ten percent of their total potential. Even those who are considered great leaders utilize only fifteen to twenty percent of their capabilities.

Your level of achievement, therefore, depends on one key factor — your willingness and desire. As Thomas Edison said, "If we were to do all the things we're capable of doing, we would literally astonish ourselves."

With all the qualities I have subscribed to effective leaders, one might think that they are not human. Abraham Zalenik puts it all in perspective in the first paragraph of his book *Human Dilemmas of Leadership:*

> The most self-conscious people in the world are its leaders. They may also be the most anxious and insecure. As men of action, leaders face risks and uncertainty, and often display remarkable courage in shouldering grave responsibility. But beneath their fortitude, there often lies an agonizing sense of doubt and a need to justify themselves.

One final question needs to be addressed: Is the profession of leadership, with all its inherent problems, toil and tribulation, worth the effort? The answer, of course, depends on your

From the little spark may burst a mighty flame.

Dante

perspective. If you take the broad view, in terms of what the leader can do to make people feel good about themselves and help them succeed, there is no question about the value of the profession. A leader in management has the opportunity to influence his or her subordinates and associates for more than half of their waking hours. **What an opportunity to serve others and help shape the future of mankind!**

XII

The Ten Commandments
of Leadership

The Ten Commandments of Leadership

I   TREAT EVERYONE WITH RESPECT AND DIGNITY.

II   SET THE EXAMPLE FOR OTHERS TO FOLLOW.

III   BE AN ACTIVE COACH.

IV   MAINTAIN THE HIGHEST STANDARDS OF HONESTY AND INTEGRITY.

V   INSIST ON EXCELLENCE AND HOLD YOUR PEOPLE ACCOUNTABLE.

VI   BUILD GROUP COHESIVENESS AND PRIDE.

VII   SHOW CONFIDENCE IN YOUR PEOPLE.

VIII   MAINTAIN A STRONG SENSE OF URGENCY.

IX   BE AVAILABLE AND VISIBLE TO YOUR STAFF.

X   DEVELOP YOURSELF TO YOUR HIGHEST POTENTIAL.

SECRETS OF EFFECTIVE LEADERSHIP
can be used in a variety of ways
to develop the leadership skills
of your management team. Some
suggestions:

- Distribute the book to supervisors and managers with a
  cover letter.

- Hand it out at management
  conferences.

- Use it in conjunction with
  management training
  programs.

Quantity discounts are available for
orders from 3 to 1000 books. For
information write:

Director of Marketing
Leadership Education
and Development, Inc.
1116 West 7th Street
Suite 175,
Columbia, TN. 38401

Available in hard bound editions.

References

INTRODUCTION

John Naisbitt, *Megatrends* (New York: Warner Books, Inc., 1982), p. 57.

I   WHAT IS LEADERSHIP

1. Mary Parker Follett, *Dynamic Administration* (New York: Harper & Row Publishers, 1941), p. 143.

2. Robert Levering, Milton Moskowitz and Michael Katz, *The 100 Best Companies To Work For In America* (New York: New American Library, 1985), p. 110.

3. Baldwin H. Ward, ed., *The Great Innovators* (New York: Year Inc., 1970), p. 157.

4. John Naisbitt and Patricia Aburdene, *Re-inventing the Corporation* (New York: Warner Books, Inc., 1985), p. 24.

5. Harold Geneen, *Managing* (Garden City: Doubleday and Company, Inc., 1984), p. 146.

III THE DEVELOPMENT OF LEADERSHIP STYLE
Dwight D. Eisenhower, *At Ease: Stories I Tell To Friends* (New York: Doubleday and Company, Inc., 1967), p. 136.

IV PROFILE OF AN EFFECTIVE LEADER
1. Bruce Catton, *The Army of the Potomac: A Stillness at Appomattox* (Garden City: Doubleday and Company, Inc., 1953), p. 44.

2. *Ibid.*, p. 46.

3. Thomas F. O'Boyle and Terence Roth, "War and Peace," *The Wall Street Journal*, September 7, 1985.

4. *Ibid.*

1. THE EFFECTIVE LEADER BUILDS GROUP COHESIVENESS AND PRIDE
1. Jack Brennan, "Patriots Grateful for Berry," *The Commercial Appeal*, January 14, 1986.

2. Warren Bennis and Bert Nanus, *Leaders* (New York: Harper & Row, Publishers, 1985), p. 30.

2. THE EFFECTIVE LEADER LIVES BY THE HIGHEST STANDARDS OF HONESTY AND INTEGRITY
1. "Managers Rank Competence and Integrity as Most Desired Values," *Management Review*, September, 1982.

2. *Bits and Pieces*, October, 1985.

3. Thomas F. O'Boyle, "More 'Honesty' Tests Used to Gauge Worker's Morale," *Wall Street Journal*, July 11, 1985.

4. Morgan W. McCall, Jr. and Michael M. Lombardo, "What Makes A Top Executive?" *Psychology Today*, February, 1983.

5. Robert S. Wieder, "Dr. Truth," *Success*.

6. *Ibid.*

7. Kenneth Blanchard and Norman Vincent Peale, *The Power of Ethical Management* (New York: Fawcett Crest, 1988), p. 20.

8. The Rotary International Motto.

9. Blanchard and Peale, *The Power of Ethical Management,* p. 20.

4. THE EFFECTIVE LEADER COACHES TO IMPROVE PERFORMANCE
Board Room Reports, April, 1985. (Interview with Mary Kay Ash).

5. THE EFFECTIVE LEADER INSISTS ON EXCELLENCE
1. *Board Room Reports,* October 15, 1986.
2. ''Bringing Out the Best In People,'' *Reader's Digest,* October, 1986.
3. Alan Loy McGinnis, *Bringing Out the Best In People* (Minneapolis: Augsburg Publishing House, 1985), p. 98.
4. Blanchard and Peale, *The Power of Ethical Management,* p. 122.

6. THE EFFECTIVE LEADER SETS THE EXAMPLE FOR OTHERS TO FOLLOW
1. *Wall Street Journal,* May 30, 1984. (Advertisement by Shearson Lehman American Express.)
2. Hal Bodley, ''From First Big-League Hit To The 3999th, Rose and Co. Remember,'' *USA Today,* April 11, 1984.
3. ''Tom Watson Looks At The Past And The Present,'' *The Wall Street Journal,* April 7, 1986.
4. *Bits and Pieces,* October, 1985.
5. Bennis and Nanus, *Leaders,* p. 70.
6. *Ibid.*
7. John T. Molloy, *Molloy's Live For Success* (New York: Bantam Books, 1983), p. 2.
8. Naisbitt and Aburdene, p. 85.
9. Michael Korda, ''Ten Steps to Success Before 40,'' *Reader's Digest,* December, 1989.

8. THE EFFECTIVE LEADER HAS COURAGE
Jackie Robinson, *Baseball Has Done It* (Philadelphia: J. B. Lippincott Company, 1944).

11. THE EFFECTIVE LEADER HAS A STRONG SENSE OF URGENCY
Edward V. Rickenbacker, *Rickenbacker* (Englewood Cliffs: Prentice-Hall, Inc., 1967), p. 400.

12. THE EFFECTIVE LEADER MAKES EVERY MINUTE COUNT
1. *The Wall Street Journal of Management,* (Homewood, Illinois: Dow Jones-Irwin Inc., 1985), p.6. Article by Andrew S. Grove, ''Your Most Precious Resource: Your Time.''
2. Brain S. Moskal, ''No Interruptions, Please!'' *Industry Week,* October 13, 1986.

15. THE EFFECTIVE LEADER LISTENS TO SUBORDINATES
    James MacGregor Burns, *Leadership* (New York: Harper & Row, Publishers, 1978).

16. THE EFFECTIVE LEADER IS DETERMINED
    1. *Time,* February 21, 1983.
    2. Ward, p. 90.
    3. Geoffrey C. Ward, "How Teddy Roosevelt Took Charge," *Success.*
    4. Peggy Reisser, "Churchill Casts A Long Shadow," *The Commercial Appeal,* September 17, 1985.

17. THE EFFECTIVE LEADER IS AVAILABLE AND VISIBLE TO HIS OR HER SUBORDINATES
    David Ogilvy, *"Leadership—The Forgotten Factor In Management."* (A Charles Coolidge Parlin Memorial Lecture, May 10, 1972).

VI HOW TO KEEP YOUR HEALTH BY MANAGING STRESS
    1. Sally Ann Stewart, "Burnout Woes? Join the Crowd," *USA Today,* December 23, 1985.
    2. *USA Today,* January 22, 1986.
    3. Herbert Benson and Robert L. Allen, "How Much Stress Is Too Much?" *Harvard Business Review,* September-October, 1980.
    4. *Bottom Line-Personal,* April 30, 1984.
    5. *Future Focus — Advancement and Leadership Strategies,* (Industry Week, 1984), p. 53. Article by Perry Pascarella, "What Makes A Good Manager."
    6. Dr. Lee Salk, "The Other Side of Retirement Planning," *Bottom Line-Personal,* June 30, 1986.
    7. Ralph LaForge, "Exercise, Self-Esteem, and the Mini-Boost," *Executive Health,* January, 1987.
    8. *Bottom Line-Personal,* February 15, 1986 and *U.S.A. Today,* February 7, 1986.
    9. *Bottom Line-Personal,* March 15, 1984.

10. Benson and Allen, p. 87.

11. *Bottom Line-Personal,* March 30, 1984.

12. Jonathon D. Brown, *Bottom Line-Personal,* April 30, 1987.

13. *Bottom Line-Personal,* September 30, 1985. (From study at Harvard University published in the *Journal of the American Medical Association.*)

14. *Bottom Line-Personal,* January 20, 1984.

15. Mary Powers, "Breaking The Habit Called Best For Life," *The Commercial Appeal,* November 18, 1965.

16. *Business Week,* January 27, 1986.

17. *Runner's World,* February, 1982.

18. *Ibid.*

19. *Bottom Line-Personal,* September 15, 1985. (From Stanford University study cited in *Men's Health.*)

20. *Bottom Line-Personal,* January 30, 1984.

21. Paul G. Engel, "Unwinding — How CEOs Escape the Pressures of Business," *Industry Week,* December 20, 1985.

22. *Ibid.*

23. *Bottom Line-Personal,* August 15, 1985.

24. *Bits and Pieces,* July, 1982.

25. Ann Reilly Dowd, "What Managers Can Learn From Manager Reagan," *Fortune,* September 15, 1986.

26. Denis Waitley, *Seeds of Greatness* (Old Tappan: Fleming H. Revell Co., 1983), p. 162.

VII   STRIVING FOR A MORE SATISFYING PERSONAL LIFE

1. *Bottom Line-Personal,* June 30, 1986.

2. *Bottom Line-Personal,* August 30, 1985.

3. Leo F. Buscaglia, PhD., "On the Challenges of Relationships," *Executive Health Report,* December, 1986.

4. *Bottom Line-Personal,* October, 1986.

5. *Reader's Digest,* March, 1988.

6. *Board Room Reports,* April 1, 1988. *(From Secrets of Strong Families by Dr. Nick Stinnett.)*

7. Keven P. Phillips, ''Reagan's America — A Capital Offence,'' *The New York Times Magazine,* June 17, 1990.

8. Waitley, p. 100.

VIII   LEADERSHIP SKILL DEVELOPMENT — A LIFE-TIME PURSUIT

1. Bennis and Nanus, p. 59.

2. *Ibid,* p. 188.

XIII

Index

A

A&P (Great Atlantic and Pacific Tea
    Company), 9
Accountability
   of subordinates, 63-66
Advances in Experimental Social Psychology, 88
Allen, James, 181
American Cancer Society. 121
American Management Association, 32
American Medical Association, 115
Anatomy of an Illness, 128
Arcastle, Virginia, 182
Aristotle, 127
Armour, Philip, 180
Ash, Mary Kay, 46
Availability
   to your Staff, 102-105

B

Bailey, Bonnie, 117
Baker, Dr. Larry, 81
Balance in life
   how to maintain, 117-119
Balboa, Rocky, 62
Baltimore Colts, 58
Bannish, Roger, 49
Barton, Bruce, 69, 177
Baruch, Bernard M., 185
Basic Management Handbook, 48
Bass, Art, 155
Bate, 184
Bay of Pigs, 96
Beaumont, 175
Beecher, Henry Ward, 138, 184
Behavior change
   encouraging/reinforcing, 63-66
Belker, L. B., 38
Bennett, Jr., Lerone, 4
Bennis, Warren, 71, 147
Berry, Raymond, 25, 58
The Best of Success, 187
Bismark, 185
Bits and Pieces, 60, 125
Bittle, Less, 38
Blily, Lynn, 28
Bly, Nelli, 100
Boardman, G. D., 176
Bohr, Niels, 180
Borman, Frank, 71, 93

"Breakthru", 101
Brennan College Services, Incorporated, 64
Bringing Out the Best in People, 47
Brooklyn Dodgers, 68
Brothers, Dr. Joyce, 186
Brown, Dr. Jonathon D., 120
Bruyers, 177
Buddha, 186
Burke, Edmond, 46
Burns, James MacGregor, 96
Butler, Samuel, 55

C

Cardinals, 68
Carlson, Ed., 102
Carlyle, Thomas, 178
Carney, Dennis J., 23
Carson Pirie Scott, Incorporated, 25
Center for Creative Leadership, 34
Channing, William Ellery, 173, 177
Charisma, 100
Chrysler Corporation, 68
Churchran, Tom, 39-40
Churchill, Winston, 7, 62, 100, 173, 177
Cicero, 67
Coaching
   to improve performance, 41-47
Coaching for Improved Work Performance, 30, 44
Cohesiveness
   group, 25-31
Communicating
   with employees, 38-40
Complacency
   how to avoid, 77
Confidence
   showing it in subordinates, 71
Confucius, 47
Conner, General Fox, 17
Conroy, Dr. Robert W., 134
Control
   of personal life, 117-119
Coolidge, Calvin, 99
Courage, 67-70
Cousins, Norman: *Anatomy of an Illness,* 128
Critical success areas, 78-79
Cuban missile crisis, 96
Cubs, 68
Curie, Madame, 134